Finding Home

A Creative Journey
on a Trip Around
the World

To Dean

The world is but a canvas to the imagination.
Henry David Thoreau

I want to be all that I am capable of becoming.
Katherine Mansfield

Contents

✤ Prologue ✤

Scruffy backpackers on giant posters smile back at me. Groups of travellers, probably fresh out of college, tilt their heads together for the camera while trekking through the wild outdoors. I imagine them climbing mountain peaks and barreling over crazy rapids, or putting themselves in danger from animal attacks and subzero temperatures. They feel at home in places that require expert camping skills to survive, and somehow manage to survive in the rugged countryside with local tribes and strange foods.

I am not one of those people, and probably never will be. After all, I am afraid of heights, fast-moving rapids, and get squeamish around too much red meat. But if I was more adventurous and brave, could I be one of those people? Is it possible to change through travel?

Conversations about packaged tours and dream trips fill the office as other young men and women linger around with high hopes to escape the city. Travel agents enthusiastically point out options for flights, accommodation and sightseeing. They conveniently tuck everything into a neat take-away package, complete with business cards and company brochures – eye candy for the wanna-be traveller. All your hopes and dreams in two weeks of paid vacation happiness.

My husband Dean and I wait for our agent to investigate all of our options for flights around the world. She clicks away at her keyboard, studies the monitor, and clicks away some more. A world map fills the entire wall beside us, and my eyes dart to all the countries we've planned so far. All of this feels like a really cool movie, and we are the stars. Rather than tell people that I work in an office, I can now add "future world traveller" to my life resume. It's something I can actually feel proud of, something that people will envy, which seems odd to me after feeling like wallpaper for so many years.

What the hell are we doing? Are we crazy? I look back at Dean, the more courageous of us, and feel grateful for his support. I feel overwhelmed thinking about all the preparation involved, but it also gives me a strong sense of purpose. Maybe I'm a different version of those young travellers hanging on the wall.

Our agent looks up from her computer and begins explaining the options for round-the-world flight packages. Keeping in mind our planned itinerary for the year, *Package A* appears to be the best fit. She prints out the multi-page document for us to analyze all the logistics.

We ask her if any changes can be made once we book, but she shakes her head. "Not without a penalty, and can you imagine trying to make a change in a country like Thailand? Better to finalize it now, and stick with your plans," she says.

This is it. By signing this document, there is no backing out.

❧ Chapter One ❧
An Opened Candy Jar

One year earlier

TORONTO, CANADA

I'm alone in the small, cramped office. My boss and co-worker have already left for the day, leaving early to beat the bulge of commuter traffic back home, and I have two more hours to go. I've just finished the last few e-mails and membership entries, and my plastic inbox tray is now empty. I consider sneaking out a bit early, but then my mind wanders off into a dull daze.

I stare at the crowded stack of binders and forms waiting to be filed into chronological order. On the pale grey walls hang a collection of event posters showcasing the achievements of our organization, a constant reminder of what I'm supposed to be passionate about. Luckily I have the freedom to select my own inspiring images for desktop wallpaper, which is often a continuous cycle of Roxy Quiksilver surfers riding steep ocean waves.

It's not supposed to be like this. The reason I went back to university was to get a full-time job I enjoyed. I had so much faith in my education, so much hope for a more creative life focusing on sport and recreation. Wanting to carry over my enthusiasm for a healthy lifestyle, I dreamed about being in a position of inspiring the public and creating programs that promoted these ideals.

But all this paper shuffling and data entry drudgery is creating a gap between my ideals and career reality. The straightforward, repetitive tasks suppress any urge for creativity, and over time speed and efficiency have taken over as a way to feel challenged.

I check the clock, and only ten minutes have passed. I can't stand being here anymore. *Why can't anyone hear me? I need more than this!* I know I'm capable of more than organizing club forms and updating records.

I load up a new Word document on my laptop and type "What do I want?" at the top of the page. I even select an offbeat font – Chiller – to make it more interesting. Once I start typing, each statement flows right into the next.

I want energy

I want positive spirit

I want artistic freedom

I want to be set free and fly around the world

I want to experience a bigger, more fulfilling life

Could this actually come true? Not in my lifetime. These are lofty goals. Flying around the world is something that only the very rich, or extremely resourceful people do.

But it's a nice idea, like dreaming about winning the lottery, and something to pass the time.

I print off the page, read it over for accuracy, and fold it up to take home. It's my little secret. I can't risk my co-workers finding these life goals on my desk. I need to look like a joiner – not someone who wants to escape and travel the world.

I glance over at the clock and smile. I pack up my empty lunch containers, water bottle and yoga magazine, and get the heck out of there.

@

The chaos of trying to find my true calling, as so many career books enthusiastically promote, leads me to a counsellor who promises just that. After years of struggling I am desperate for someone else to wave their magic wand – their spark of inspiration miraculously landing the perfect occupation in my lap.

Over several sessions Carol guides me through a series of exercises reflecting on my skills, work preferences and dreams for the future. She confirms that I have "artistic tendencies" but am not necessarily an artist. I fight hard to not argue her point, but then wonder if it's actually true.

Carol asks me to write down my favourite careers and how I envision myself in them. "Actress" makes the top of the list, and I compose a scene of my new life as a successful performer, working with prestigious directors and other talented actors. A sense of relief fills my body, but then becomes saturated with restlessness and nervous energy. A million other career options tempt me, and soon confusion puts a halt to any further progress. I desperately want adventure, but don't know what form that would take.

Then Carol asks me, "What if you and Dean sell your house and travel around the world?"

My stomach tightens as I stare back at her. She begins to rationalize how Dean and I both appear to need a change, and this could be the perfect solution. Dean's job in television is also becoming a grind, and his dream of working as a news cameraman after college is spiraling downward. However a trip around the world won't solve these problems. I quickly toss the suggestion away, and attempt to steer the conversation to more practical ideas.

On the streetcar ride home, I read over all the exercises in my binder notes. Carol's odd question keeps popping in my head. I try to brush it off, but it sinks deeper in my mind. *What if we did travel the world? No, don't be stupid. Dean would never agree to that. Stop thinking about it. But what if...it would be great to.....stop! Stop! STOP!*

While Dean cooks dinner I ponder how to sneak the question into our conversation. I set the table to keep my fidgets to a minimum, and once dinner is ready, help carry the spaghetti and salads to the table. Dean takes off his hoodie and tosses it on the couch, an attempt to strip away the demands of a long workday. I sit down and take a few bites of food, trying to remain calm while my mind races through a million possible ways to introduce the topic.

"So, Carol was thinking that it might be a good idea for us to travel around the world. She said we could sell our house and travel for a year," I say, biting my lip afterward.

Dean pauses for a moment and says, "That would be great, but I don't think we can really do that right now. I'm set in my job, and getting a year off would likely be impossible."

I nod in agreement, and twirl the pasta around my fork. I look back at Dean, who's focused solely on his plate of food, and ask him about his day at work.

@

On a mild evening in early October we decide to see a movie, and perhaps go for drinks afterwards. Dean recently finished reading the book *Into the Wild*, and wanted to see the screen version with his cousin Richard. At the last minute I agree to tag along, unsure if I will enjoy a story about a young guy who ventures off to the Alaskan wilderness. Seems like a "man versus the elements" kind of guy flick, but maybe there will be some impressive landscape shots.

We take the streetcar and subway up to Cumberland Theatre and meet Richard in the lobby. After sifting through the ticket booth we are drawn to the sound of sloshing drinks and crackling popcorn at the snack counter. The young man pours a hefty scoop of buttered corn into the glossy bag, complemented with an ice-cold pop, and we head upstairs to the theatre. I follow Richard and Dean into a row of seats near the back and relax into the velveteen chair.

As I watch the story of Christopher McCandless gradually unfold, I begin to understand his strong desire to escape and challenge himself through long-term travel. Christopher's adventures start small, winding his way around to some of America's small towns and countryside, and gradually increase in difficulty until reaching his final destination in Alaska. His travel experiences and the people he meets along the way help shape his attitude about the beauty of nature and the pleasure of living a simple, materialistic-free way of life.

Once the credits start rolling I lead the way out of the theatre. My fingertips are still tingling from the movie's dramatic ending, and I immediately want to confirm with Dean to see if he feels the same.

I turn around and whisper, "That was a great movie. Did you like it?"

"Yeah, it was really good. Powerful message too," he says.

The three of us stroll down Spadina Avenue to meet a few other friends at the local pub, The Ferret and Firkin. The air is cool but refreshing, and I hold Dean's hand to keep it warm.

We reserve a table outside on the patio, and then head inside to place our order. While perched on bar stools, we both comment on the bravery of Christopher McCandless. Even in the most extreme living conditions he stayed true to his values and genuine love of nature.

A few seconds later I ask Dean, "What if we tried something really big?"

Dean lights up and says, "Yeah, what if we traveled for a year?"

"A trip around the world – for a year!" we say almost simultaneously.

We grin like schoolchildren at the start of summer. The excitement spirals up to my head, which surprises me since I haven't started drinking yet. Suddenly our future begins to sparkle as it takes off into flight. We whisper ideas back and forth while protectively glancing around the bar. The bartender hands us two pints of beer and we go join our friends on the patio.

"Don't say anything. Pretend that nothing happened!" I giggle to Dean on the way out.

Conversations spill around me as I try to keep the biggest secret on Earth. My body is sitting in a plastic chair, but my mind floats away into a world of adventure. All the meaningless chatter, sarcastic jokes, workplace gossip and political debates between the guys don't bother me at all. I could care less, because Dean and I are about to plan the most thrilling, fulfilling, life-changing trip of the century. Everything else is just filler.

After the last sip of beer, and everyone checks their watches to gauge the last train home, we each throw in a twenty to cover the bill. The waitress collects the filmy glasses onto her tray and wishes us a good night. If only she knew our night was just beginning. We take the Spadina streetcar downtown and across King to get us back to our cozy townhouse.

We barrel up the steep stairs to our living room. I immediately rush around the entire house to find our Map of the World, feeling a little lightheaded but focused. I flip through piles of papers and books in our office, wishing that we had cleaned up the mess earlier in the closet.

"I found it!" I scream while running back down to the living room.

I unfold the map and smooth it out on the floor. While Dean looks it over I grab a notebook and pen to record the results.

"Which countries do we want to travel to?" I ask.

The whole world is like an opened candy jar, and we're plunging in for the best treats.

"Australia of course, New Zealand…" I start to say while writing.

"Southeast Asia for sure, Europe…" Dean says as he points to the countries with his finger.

The flow of our conversation is natural and easy, as if subconsciously we'd been planning this trip for months. I quickly jot down the country names, and create a basic itinerary for an entire year of travel.

❧ Chapter Two ❧

Diving In

CAIRNS, AUSTRALIA

We arrive at Caravella Backpackers in mid-afternoon, and are immediately greeted with an enthusiastic welcome in that enviable "I just got back from surfing" Aussie accent. The reception walls are filled with posters advertising packaged adventure tours throughout Queensland, attracting a crowd of scruffy heads and slick bikini girls mingling around the front desk.

Once checked in, the staff invite us to rest our backpacks in the dining area while the cleaning crew put the final touches on our room. Surrounding the property are two-story cottages painted in soft violet, accented with turquoise blue window frames. Beach towels and swimsuits are clipped to a clothesline in front of several coin laundry machines. A colourful sign advertising Pro Dive Cairns hangs above the kitchen with cartoon drawings of scuba divers swimming around tropical fish and sea turtles.

The main attraction is the large, sun-sparkled pool decorated with tiles in Mediterranean blue. Around the perimeter lie a string of sunbathers stretched out on angled loungers, arms stretched long and feet flopped open. Several women are perched along the edge of the pool, stomachs pulled in, teasing the water with gentle kicks toward their captive male audience. None of them look a day older than twenty-five.

Dean bears the load of the backpack as I slip my arms out of the damp, padded straps. We rest our packs beside a picnic table and slump down onto the bench, wiping strands of hair away from our dewy foreheads. I feel overdressed in my cargo pants and t-shirt, now clinging with sweat expanding down my back.

After a long year of endless tasks filled with research, travel bookings, medical appointments, selling our townhouse and boxing up everything into storage, followed by 22 hours on three different flights sitting in cramped economy-class seats, my brain hasn't adjusted to the fact that our trip has now begun. *I don't know if I'm ready to start a life without regular schedules and familiar faces. What if I screw it up?*

Just two days ago we hugged goodbye to our families, and a tearful farewell to our cats staying with my parents. I'd spent the last six months proving to people that everything was under control and could handle a trip of this magnitude. It was easy to get caught up in the business of travel planning and logistics, backed up with a continuous surge of admiration from friends and co-workers. Besides a few hiccups it was all going as planned, complete with a farewell party a week before our departure.

However the last few moments before leaving I questioned whether I was ready to go. There were no more bookings or visa applications to take care of, no more supplies to shop for, no more visits to health clinics for last minute check-ups. My stomach churned as my mind created an endless cycle of doubts, alarming me of all the potential flaws and mishaps that could happen. Like a nervous actor, I couldn't relax until the show began. I reminded myself to take it one step at a time. All we had to do was get on a plane and let the magic begin.

"How long do you think it will be?" I ask Dean, anxiously waiting for our room to be ready.

"Why don't you see if the door is open?" he says.

I leave Dean to guard the packs while I aim to get a sneak preview of our room. Along the way I pass by the communal kitchen. Mini stove stations sit on top of a white-tiled countertop with pots and pans tucked underneath, and cleaning ladies are scrubbing forgotten dishes beside the sink. A large fridge sits off to the side with a list of rules taped to the door. I remind myself to check out the "community food" cupboard for leftover pasta, spices and other handy ingredients we could use later for meals.

The stone pathway winds around the cottages and I find a lime green painted sign for Room #66. The door is open, so I peer inside and immediately notice the smooth, warm glow of the wood floors. Sunlight shines through gauzy blue drapes in the sitting area, and I can already imagine eating our morning breakfast in this cozy room. The bedroom is large for a hostel, with an iron rod double bed sitting in the middle of the room, and a drying rack that will be perfect for hanging up laundry or a wet bikini.

A small refrigerator in the corner of the room brings a sigh of relief, knowing that I won't have to store our food in the overstuffed communal fridge in between opened boxes of frozen dinners, canned soup, a pot of macaroni that has noodles permanently stuck to the sides, and bits of expired food filling the cracks. Just a hunch, but given the young crowd hanging around the pool, I'm guessing that they're not all gourmet cooks.

I turn around and see a sparkling clean bathroom with deep yellow, blue and white tiles decorating the walls and floor. A large shower stall, modern pedestal sink and toilet complete the feeling of comfort and convenience. I run back to Dean to tell him the good news, feeling proud of how everything is working out perfectly so far.

When I return Dean is already holding the key in his hand, so we carry our packs to the room. He throws his bag down onto the floor and heads outside while I carefully set mine on the bed and begin unpacking, wondering how all my clothes survived the long flight. The feeling of panic I had after selling our house and bunking with family like lost souls has now lost its grip, and is replaced with a new sense of what *home* means.

Rather than exclusively a place that has my name attached to it, *home* will be the spot I rest my pack in our temporary room. It'll be my favourite sundress and t-shirts carefully selected for the trip, and the way Dean wraps his arms around me after a long day. *Home* will be doing the things I love, from strolling through art galleries to a rejuvenating yoga routine. *Home* will be a sense of peace within a whirlwind of excitement.

I join Dean out on the patio, where the pool sits waiting for me to dive in. Craving its cool water, I instead lie motionless on the plastic lounge chair, heavy from exhaustion. I take a deep breath, settling in to my new role as "World Traveller". Dean is stretched out on the lounger beside me, eyes drifting close, still smiling from the fact that he's away from work for an entire year and about to visit some of the most amazing places on Earth.

@

"You can do this. Just tell her we have a few questions about scuba courses. She looks really friendly," Dean says.

I look over at the young blonde woman wearing O'Neill sportswear and organizing goggles at the front desk. Tusa Dive doesn't seem as overwhelming as some of the other scuba shops downtown, so Dean thought it would be a good place to start our interviews. I flip open my notebook and scan over the questions we discussed this morning at the hostel. But then I look up at all the strange nozzles and tubes and dials hanging on the walls.

"I'll just look around the store first," I say to Dean.

"Just go talk to her. She'll answer all your questions about merchandise and stuff."

"All right, fine."

I walk over to the desk like I'm about to go on stage. Meanwhile Dean is busy planning our next interviews and where to submit stories for travel articles. His natural aptitude for freelance work is inspiring, and I try to keep up with his enthusiasm by following his lead. After all he's the photographer and I can write, and we both love to travel. So it's a natural fit, right?

This master plan was also part of the pitch to my parents when we presented our crazy idea to travel the world for a year, hoping that they would be willing to take care of our cats during that time. The major logistics had already been worked out to ease any concerns of financial stability. Although I would have to quit my job, Dean had confirmed arrangements for a year's leave of absence, and funding for the trip would be entirely through the sale of our house.

As a highly organized and practical person, it was important to my dad that we have an objective for how to apply all the new experiences we would gain on the trip. Simply wanting to be adventurous and see exotic cultures wasn't enough. Dean had already set up a website for us to post updates during our trip, appropriately named *Backpack Adventures*, which began the process of our new life as a husband and wife travel team.

Dean shared with my dad potential ideas on how to create a new career path that involved creating books and becoming travel experts. They sat on the edge of their seats debating these ideas, choosing which ones had the steepest potential: Ecotourism, adventure travel, world trips on a budget or travelling as a married couple. It all sounded very exciting as I sat nervously on the couch spinning my wedding ring, wondering what kind of person I'd have to become to make this entrepreneurial dream a reality.

I smile at the Sales Associate, hoping that my friendly face can overcome any embarrassing fumbles that will likely happen in the next thirty seconds.

"Hi, my name is Vicki Bradley. I'm a travel writer. Can I ask you some questions about scuba diving?"

"Sure, what would you like to know?" she says.

I look down at my notebook for the first question, and begin a series of inquiries about instructor qualifications, diving experience for participants, and the various packages they offer. As she responds I try to keep a memory of her answers in my mind, not wanting to disrupt the conversation with my slow note-taking skills. As a potential consumer I feel reassured that all scuba packages in Queensland must follow strict guidelines for safety, and other than minimum health standards, participants do not need any prior diving experience.

"Do you have any other questions?" she asks.

I look down at my list, not really seeing the questions, and reply, "No that's everything, thanks."

I turn to Dean, who reminds me to get her name before we leave.

"Excuse me, can I get your name please?"

"It's Chantelle."

"Great, thanks!"

I motion to Dean to leave quickly so I can breathe again. We find a park bench down the street, and I collapse in a huff.

"You did great! See, it's not that bad, is it? It just takes practice, that's all," Dean says, and then adds, "I was thinking we should go over to the Cairns Tourism Board to see if we can get an interview there."

With his wide eyes and big smile, I agree to keep going. *Maybe it will get easier with time.*

Luckily the downtown core of Cairns is fairly condensed, making it easy to find the Tourism office. The décor and staff have the same laid-back Aussie attitude as the locals, and our meeting is more like a casual get together than a formal interview. Wearing a Hawaiian-style shirt and offering us cookies in their small meeting room, the Marketing rep immediately makes us feel at ease.

This time I'm letting Dean take the spotlight with all the questions, and I'll fill in for support. I'm more interested in the colourful Great Barrier Reef posters hanging on the walls, and my mind wanders as I gaze at the images. *What a beautiful place to work! I wonder if they get discounts, or better yet free tours of the reef and rainforests? I want to live in this tropical paradise!* I glance over at Dean, who's taking notes during the interview, and feel grateful that one of us is paying attention.

Following the informative conversation about eco-friendly tourism, we make one more stop – Pro Dive Cairns. The afternoon is scorching hot now, but we're energized to keep going. With all the information we've gathered so far, we agree that the article will focus on the Eco Certified program and its effect on consumers when choosing tour packages in sensitive natural environments.

The Marketing Manager for Pro Dive Cairns welcomes Dean and I with a big smile and leads us into his office. We sit across from his desk, and I open my notebook ready to record like a secretary. I smile at Dean, waiting for him to start the conversation with Mr. Scuba Man. With his naturally sociable personality, Dean looks like a professional journalist. He has all the right questions and isn't afraid to ask for clarification on anything he doesn't understand. I scribble down a few key terms and statistics, but most of the time my eyes glaze over all the data and other important details I should be interested in.

After the interview we are invited to watch part of a scuba class in their training pool. I watch closely to see how the people in the class manage all that heavy equipment, and breathing with an air tank strapped to their backs. Each participant takes turns to sink down into the water while the others watch from above. Waves of jitters flow through my body as I imagine myself in a beginner's class trying to learn how to survive underwater. After a few minutes we thank the staff for their generosity and leave the facility with many more facts to add to our article.

Back at the hostel we try to combine all of our information into a coherent piece. Suddenly writing feels like a foreign language, like I'm writing an essay for an Environmental Studies class. No creativity needed here. My mind has already pulled away from this project – a combination of fear and confusion – and I let Dean take over. I look out the window at all the people gathered around the pool, and desperately want to dolphin dive to the bottom of the pool, blocking out all the noise from above.

@

While researching the downtown neighbourhood for dive shops, Dean and I discover barbecue grilling stations along the waterfront. Several pavilions are set up next to the boardwalk, each equipped with a stone counter that holds two large metal pans for grilling. Dean's eyes immediately light up at all the possible opportunities for cooking meat in the great outdoors. So with grocery list in hand, we walk to a downtown supermarket to stock up on food.

For many years I've admired Dean's talent for cooking, and his creativity with limited resources. With only basic ingredients like chicken, a tomato, green pepper and a couple jars of herbs, Dean can whip up a gourmet meal in minutes. Although I've joked with people that I married Dean for his cooking skills, it's a wonderful asset that I feel very fortunate to benefit from. And what's sexier than a man cooking a gourmet meal for his wife or girlfriend?

Dean also loves to try new foods, and virtually any meat is fair game. While I choose the more conventional option of salmon fillet, Dean ventures toward kangaroo steak. I try not to think about the life of Kanga or Roo as Dean drops the packaged meat into the cart. We round out the meal with potatoes, a salad and bottle of wine, and walk back to the hostel with two full bags of dinner ingredients. We also picked up essentials like cereal (the more fibre the better), a small container of milk, bread, peanut butter, granola bars, fruit and veggies, and a pre-cooked chicken.

Dean prepares the steak by rubbing a few cloves of garlic on the dark brown meat, and adds some turmeric, pepper and orange-coloured spice he discovers in the hostel kitchen. He tops it off with a drizzle of olive oil and a few slices of red onion. While I chop up veggies for a salad, Dean prepares a papaya and strawberry salsa mixture for my salmon. We borrow some plates and cutlery from the hostel, and use plastic baggies to carry the food down to the waterfront.

After several attempts of trying to turn on the barbecue, Dean finally gets it going. He carefully places the kangaroo steak and salmon on the metal pans, and smiles proudly while the food sizzles in response. We share the grilling station with another family cooking their dinner, and watch the sky turn shades of ginger and saffron. In the distance are sailboats resting at shore for the night, their dark outlines creating a portrait of the perfect ocean lifestyle. As Dean plays Master Chef to the sizzling meat, fish and potatoes, I set out the plates and side dishes on the picnic table. I take a deep breath of the warm salty air and feel like the luckiest girl in the world.

The kangaroo steak and salmon both turn out beautifully on the barbecue. Dean scoops the food out of the metal pan onto the plates, and carries it over to the picnic table like a proud waiter. By the time everything is ready, a beautiful sunset and stars form the backdrop to our magical dinner.

GREAT BARRIER REEF

Despite having absolutely no contact with the ocean growing up, other than a few family trips to Florida, I had an unusual obsession to be a surfer. To me it looked like the coolest sport on the planet. While the rest of my family focused on more traditional Canadian pastimes like *Hockey Night in Canada*, I dreamed of surfing in California and Hawaii. I wasn't particularly adventurous, but I imagined surfing as a way to feel free and play in the ocean waves with the other cool kids.

I even planned holidays around surfing competitions. On a trip to Maui with Dean, I made sure to book it during the *Billabong Pro* in Honolua Bay, one of the most prestigious international surfing competitions for women. Elite-level surfers that I knew only by name would be performing – Layne Beachley, Keala Kennelly and Rochelle Ballard. Watching them compete in the big waves, and meeting Layne and Keala at a poster signing in a local surf shop, I felt like a star-struck girl meeting her childhood idols.

I never did fulfill those surfer dreams, but my love for the ocean has stayed with me ever since. Over the years Dean and I visited aquariums and flipped through coffee table books filled with tropical fish and coral reefs, but I still craved to see ocean life up close in the water.

Conveniently booking through Caravella Backpackers, we decide to take a 4-day "Learn to Dive" course with Pro Dive Cairns, trusting that our bodies will be ready for an activity this strenuous. However I'm still recovering from muscle cramping in my neck after our long flight to Australia, and my digestion hasn't figured out how to function normally since the trip began. I wish that my stomach would keep pace with the part of me that craves variety and stimulation, but instead it prefers a steady, predictable routine to keep things working properly. Hopefully these issues will work themselves out by the first day of class, especially given the $850 course fee we've invested for this.

Unfortunately in the next few days the problems become much worse. I try yoga and healthy foods to get things going, and then out of desperation purchase a fibre-rich bar at a drugstore. The recommended dose is a quarter piece, but it doesn't seem to do anything. So at 7:00 am the next morning, the day of our Scuba course, I try biting off a slighter bigger piece. *What's the worst that can happen?*

In less than an hour the bathroom is screaming my name. My stomach is doing back flips with all the internal commotion. After the worst of it passes, I lay in bed next to Dean with one hand massaging my belly and the other pressed against my forehead. Dean looks at me with concerned eyes, wondering what to do next.

My instincts tell me to let it go, and try a snorkelling trip instead. Dean lovingly takes care of all the refund details while I rest in the hostel room. I am crushed and frustrated all at once. *I'll likely never get this chance again, and now it's disappearing. Why can't my body just cooperate and let me do what I want?* Dean later admits that he was nervous about trying scuba diving and wearing that awkward mouthpiece, with the added pressure of learning the sport in only a few days before heading out into the middle of the ocean.

A couple of days later we sign up for a day trip that includes snorkelling in the deep ocean and along the shoreline of an island. As newly informed tourists, we book with Passions of Paradise, a tour company with the Eco Certified Advanced accreditation. All we need to do is show up at the waterfront docks with our registrations, and for me, swallow an anti-nausea pill to avoid seasickness.

@

The first spot we arrive at on our tour is Michaelmas Cay. The boat is full of eager participants wearing wetsuits suctioned to their bodies, and all the necessary headgear for dipping your head below water. People of all skill levels are grouped together in the boat: experienced scuba divers, first-time divers, and amateur snorkellers like us. Conversations spill around us about specialized gear and other dive spots they've been to. I sit on the bench hoping that no one will question this Ontario-born girl about diving or other cool ocean sports.

A line-up of people forms at the back of the boat, and one by one they jump off the platform. The boat is bobbing up and down from the big choppy waves, but thankfully my stomach is sailing calm waters at this point.

The instructor says to me, "Hold onto your mask and take a big jump!"

Okay, seems like a simple task. I take a big leap and flop onto my stomach. A little disoriented, I resurface and see Dean's face behind his goofy goggles waiting for me to join him. Forgetting all my swimming strokes, I start dog paddling over to him.

Once within range of the group I re-adjust the snorkel tube and try looking under the water. *Wow, how beautif...cough! spurt!* Water splashes in my snorkel tube. The instructor said when this happens, say the number "two" and the water should spit out from the tube. Unfortunately the waves keep splashing more water in, so I re-surface, remove the mouthpiece, and spit the water out myself. I soon realize that I can only look down in the water for about 3-5 breaths before the next wave pours in more water.

Observing the other snorkellers dipping below the surface it appears that everyone else gets the hang of this. *Am I the only snorkel spaz in the group?* After several more attempts, I motion to Dean that I'm heading in. I dog paddle back to the boat and climb up the ladder with my large webbed feet.

Once safely back on the boat, a crewmember checks my name on a list. I peel off the fins and goggles and wait for Dean to surface. The remaining snorkellers flap around like lost fish, and gradually return in time for the lunch buffet. Dean is all smiles back on board while I sit on a bench wondering if we should have tried the scuba course instead. He puts his hand on mine, and reassures me that splashes of water kept falling down his snorkel tube as well.

The kitchen staff carry out several platters of food into the dining area. Prawns, veggies, fresh buns, and a choice of meat or vegetable pasta are on the menu today. The selection is overwhelming, but I definitely worked up an appetite this morning. Dean and I gobble down the food, hoping it will be fully digested by the time we have to jump in the water again.

For the second dive we head to a small island further out in the ocean. Thankfully, gentle waves are flowing into shore when we arrive. Flocks of seagulls appear to be having an annual convention, as the entire island is filled with feathers and lively bird banter. The tour guides warn us to stay close to the water, since the island has been designated as an eco-protected area. *That's nice, but I'm more concerned about staying away from the inevitable globs of bird poop.*

A smaller boat takes us directly to the island, and we assemble our gear on the beach. Getting in the water is tricky with flippers on, although walking backwards seems to work best. I watch the more experienced snorkellers slide their flippers on after walking up to knee-high water, so I follow their technique. Walking barefoot also prevents sand collecting inside. I re-adjust my mask and tube, and walk like a zombie into the deeper water.

No worries this time around. The waves are very gentle, and I can stay underwater for a few minutes before any water gets in my tube. I'm able to take the time to observe and appreciate the beautiful scenery. Spongy mounds of coral are squeezed together in an underwater garden – some with a maze covering their bald, round heads, and others free flowing with long tentacles shifting with the ocean currents. I swim toward giant clams breathing through their rubbery openings, decorated with ribbons of bright blue. Schools of fish in deep oranges, blues and yellows scurry from spot to spot, nibbling on food attached to the coral. *I can actually hear them nibbling!* I reach out, hoping to skim their tiny bodies, but they collectively repel and continue their journey in smooth symphony. Thoughts of missing out on scuba diving fade away as I study all the different varieties of ocean life. After a few minutes I resurface and float on my back to watch the clouds go by. I want to stay here forever.

The crew wave their arms to signal us back to the boat. *Didn't we just get here?* The group dogpaddles like a beginner swim class and climbs back on board. The snorkel tube and flippers are easy to take off, but slithering out of the wetsuit takes a bit of muscle. Feeling much lighter, we slip into our t-shirts and shorts and walk up to the front deck to claim a suntanning spot on the large mesh pods. I lie on my back and review the day in my mind for a future story. I already miss the beauty of this coral reef. The waves gently lull us into an afternoon nap, and before long we arrive at the dock, a little sunburned but full of wonderful memories.

KURANDA, AUSTRALIA

NEED TO ESCAPE AND HAVE A HOLIDAY?

Want to wake up to the birds singing?
After a great night's sleep?
Want personalized old-fashioned service, rarely seen these days?

Then a visit to the family run Kuranda Backpackers is a must. This spacious Queenslander, built in 1907, has stunning leadlight windows and rooms to cater to everybody's needs. Set on 1½ acres of spectacular tropical gardens with a relaxing pool, we can offer you tranquility!

A truly unforgettable time is waiting for you.

[As advertised by Kuranda Backpackers]

A tangle of trees and overgrown plants are growing around the hostel, making it difficult to see. The building doesn't look like the website photos, making me cringe on what lies ahead. Dean and I walk up the crumbling cement stairs to the front entrance and open the weathered door.

Once inside we peel off our backpacks, setting them down beside a lopsided upholstered chair. Scanning the room, it looks like nobody has stayed here for decades. I try to find something on the reception desk with a name or address listed on it, and then notice a business card attached to a side cabinet with yellowed scotch tape. Sure enough, it's the same information I have on my printout.

There is no sign of human life anywhere, and the smell of decades-old dust fills the air. Chairs with flattened, mismatched cushions sit like dead creatures in the TV lounge area. A large futon has a stained comforter draped over its sagging mattress pad, likely used as an extra bed or something else I'd rather not think about right now. Dean searches the property to find a staff person while I stand by the entrance with a ball of tension growing in my stomach.

A few minutes later a young man appears out of nowhere and goes behind the reception desk. Wispy brown hair nearly covers his eyes, and a thin, faded t-shirt reveals a body in need of nourishment. Scanning the dog-eared pages of his guest book he checks off our names. A computer also sits on the desk, although it was likely in its prime during the 1990s. We pay the balance of fees, which he tucks into an old tin can and places underneath the desk.

The young man asks if we need help, so I quickly take him up on the offer.

"You can carry my pack, thanks."

Heaving my pack onto his shoulder, our concierge escorts us around the pool table lounge/TV room toward the back door, where we walk up rickety wooden steps to another equally fatigued building. He holds open the screen door and takes us down a hallway that feels eerily vacant. Our room is facing us at the end of the hall, where he unlocks the door with a couple of quick turns of the wrist. Resting our bags on the floor, we're then guided downstairs to the washroom facilities.

The barn-like structure has an odd mixture of unfinished walls – the lower half is made of wood and the upper half of sheet metal. A sliver of lattice between the walls provides just enough light to see down the stairs.

With each step, I try to avoid touching the thin metal handrail. Spider webs cling in corners, and a single bulb hangs down from a wire. I wonder how many people have been taken captive at night in this dark cavern.

"There's the toilet, and next to it is the shower," the young man says.

Grit and mould line the paper-thin floor and walls, and a dark, thick ring surrounds the bottom of the toilet. There's a sharp pungent odour from chemical cleaner, likely used to cover up bathroom smells, and barely enough toilet paper for one visit. A peach-coloured toilet brush sits in the corner waiting to be used.

But next door is the strangest shower stall construction I've ever seen. Sheets of corrugated metal cover the entire stall with large screws drilled in like rows of bullets. The uneven floor has pale beige tiles and a dirty drain hole collecting bits of hair. A flimsy nylon blue shower curtain is pushed to one side. I turn to Dean, who mirrors a look of disgust and horror.

We walk back up the creaky wooden steps, and the young man leaves so we can settle in. A thin double bed lies next to the window, accompanied by a twin bed and a wood-panelled air conditioner. A large cupboard for hanging clothes is a nice feature, but sits wide open with no doors or hangers. Some of the drawers are also missing.

We sit on the hard bed and discuss our options. I can feel springs pushing up through the mattress, and quickly pull up a corner of the fitted sheet to scan for blood marks – a sure sign of bed bugs. The mattress is certainly old, but there doesn't seem to be any evidence of the nasty critters.

"Maybe we can see how it goes tonight, and then look around for something better," Dean says.

"I suppose I can handle it for one night. But the problem is that we've paid the balance of room fees already. I don't know if we can get a refund for those extra nights."

"It's only three nights. Maybe it won't be that bad."

"Maybe, but we're keeping our stuff sealed up in the packs. I don't want anything touching my clothes!"

Dean agrees, and we prop up our bags in the makeshift closet to protect them from any critters exploring at night.

An hour later we decide to head into town and forget about the Hostel of Horror. Lush green trees line the pathway, giving us welcome coolness from the hot afternoon sun. The tension in my body slowly releases as we admire the natural beauty of this rainforest town.

The town of Kuranda is easy for walking around, which takes a total of ten minutes if you don't stop to browse in the shops. But shopping is the main entertainment, and storeowners are eager to show us their specialty, one-of-a-kind pieces made by local artists. Walking down the main street we discover many stores selling tropical-style silk paintings, safari wear and opal jewellery.

I step inside a large gallery shop, intrigued by patterns of colourful dots swirling around each other on many of the paintings. The patterns create representations of nature: streams, lizards, animal tracks, and people gathered around in circles. The dotted shapes ripple out to the edges of the painting like sound waves. It is the most beautiful form of abstract art I've ever seen. Having tried still life painting back home, I long to create art with greater meaning and complex patterns. The salesperson informs me that all the art is made in local aboriginal communities. My heart balloons with admiration for these talented artists, which I so desperately want to be.

Past the galleries and tourist shops are wildlife parks that feature many creatures in the Kuranda Rainforest, including the Venom Zoo. Panic fills my mind just thinking about all the scary snakes and spiders waiting to attack innocent visitors. The much gentler Koala Park is tempting, but behind some bushes we notice a sign for Bat Reach.

In tightly screened cages are groups of bats hanging upside down, clinging to the ceiling with their long, piercing claws. Part furry animal and part caped crusader, their vinyl-like coat is stretched at pointed angles by thin robot legs. A few are cloaked in complete hibernation from the curious crowd of people.

A woman inside the facility walks over to us with a baby bat clinging to her white t-shirt. She shows us the tiny animal up close, which appears innocent compared to the dark, mysterious creatures hanging in the cages. Behind her is a man with an even smaller bat tucked inside his hand, barely the size of two fingers.

"So what is Bat Reach?" Dean asks the woman.

"It's a rehab clinic, so we take care of injured or abandoned bats. We also educate people about bats."

"How did you get involved with this kind of work?" Dean inquires while studying the small, clinging creature.

"We're actually volunteers for Bat Reach, and they taught us how to take care of the animals. We feed and clean up their cages, that kind of thing. They also provide us with housing here."

"You live here?"

"Yes, we've been living in Kuranda for about a month. We're from the States. We travel around the world and stay in places for a month or two, and then move on," she explains.

"Really? We're travelling around the world too. We're just three weeks in so far."

"So you've just started – that's great! You'll have so much to experience. At some point, though, you'll hit a wall and everything will start to look the same, and you'll get tired of the grind of travelling. But then you'll experience something fantastic and want to keep going. It goes in waves. We've had that several times, but have also been to some amazing places the last couple of years."

Dean and I listen to every word, feeling like we are now part of an exclusive World Travellers Club. We're the newbies, and have just met our couples-travel mentors. After sharing a few more stories, we exchange e-mails to keep in touch.

Next we dip into The Butterfly Sanctuary near the end of Coondoo Street. Compared to all the deadly, poisonous animals that Cairns locals love talking about, butterflies are a welcome, peaceful retreat. I'm even wearing my favourite sundress in the same pattern.

The steamy greenhouse exhibit is a sanctuary of tall trees, tropical plants and trickling waterfalls, creating a luxurious environment for many species of insects. Butterflies circle around me in constant flutter, their vibrant wings glowing against the earthy colours of the exhibit. The ultramarine colour of the famous Ulysses blue butterfly stands out from the other orange and black varieties. They hover around Dean's red t-shirt, and a volunteer informs us that they mistake it for the red tropical flowers they are naturally drawn to. Chuckling at the commotion he's caused, he takes close-up photos of many species, each with their own colourful patterns.

I stroll the winding pathway, breathing in the sweet, humid air. I could easily linger for hours in this heavenly oasis, tucked in a corner all night dreaming about my new fluttery friends, and waking up with dewy skin the next morning.

Dean returns with his camera looped over his shoulder. He flips through the slideshow to double check the quality of his photos, and then hands the camera over to me. The close-up shots are an impressive duplication, but only capture the visual beauty of the exhibit. I close my eyes, and soak in the bouquet of aromas floating all around me.

On our way back to the hostel we check for better accommodation options. There is a motel across the street from the hostel, so I go inside to inquire.

"Do you have any rooms available for November 5th and 6th?"

The woman at the reception desk flips through the reservations book, and confirms that a room is available for both nights.

"Wonderful! I'd like to book that please."

"Okay, no worries. Is there a number we can reach you at?"

"No, we're actually staying at the Hostel from Hell across the street."

The receptionist stares back in shock. An older woman standing beside me chuckles and says, "So you don't recommend the place?"

"No, not at all!"

The receptionist makes note of our names, and with huge smiles we walk back to the hostel to cook dinner. We also check with the Manager about getting a refund.

"Well you put me in a difficult position. I won't be able to rent out the room on such short notice, so I can't give you a refund," he says.

Who the hell would want to stay here anyway?

Although we're sacrificing our payment for the next two nights, we feel grateful that a cozy, comfortable hotel room will be ready for our arrival tomorrow.

While we prepare our dinner – microwave meals to avoid using their rusty appliances – we notice a few other guests hanging around the common area. Two young women, barely out of their teens, are playing a game of pool with a couple scruffy older men. The women are also cooking quick-and-easy microwave meals.

"It's a good thing we're up to date on all our shots," I whisper to Dean.

I look around at the display of skin-tight skirts and prickly faces with drooping Marlboro cigarettes – an entire generation between them – slinking by each other while caressing their pool sticks. The men swig bottles of Foster's beer in between loose efforts to aim their balls towards the end pockets. Giggles of nervous laughter entice further attempts until belches and bad stories become the entertainment.

We cook our tin can meals and sneak back to the private sitting area beside our bedroom. I carefully sit down on the chair, trying not to touch my bare skin on it.

"It's just for one night. We can do this," I say to Dean.

"Yeah, but I'm actually getting scared with the thought of being here when it's dark."

Great, I hadn't thought of that. Every horror movie I've ever seen now streams through my mind.

@

A few days later we travel back on the train to Cairns and check into Caravella Backpackers until our flight leaves for Brisbane.

Today I'm alone at the hostel, but certainly not lonely. Dean is out on the ocean aboard the historical Dutch ship *Duyfken* that tourists can help sail for the day. We waved good-bye to each other at the harbour, and I returned to Caravella to rest and do some writing.

I set up the laptop on a small round table just outside our room. My creative mind is bursting with ideas for a fictional story based on the hostel in Kuranda. Although the accommodation was horrible, the extreme nature of it creates a spark of energy that I've been longing for. I plan out the basic plot of the story, the lead character and all the juicy details. I start typing and keep going until three hours later I have the horror story of the year finished. I sit back in the chair, not quite believing this writing experience, not believing that writing could be this much fun and exhilarating. I can't wait until Dean is back to share my new love.

BRISBANE, AUSTRALIA

I'm one of the first ones to arrive. A few people are sitting quietly on the sloped lawn at Rocks Riverside Park, so I roll out my mat and do a few stretches before the start of class. The soft grass cushions my thin, rubbery mat, and I gaze at the clouds above.

Anticipating that I would keep up a regular yoga routine during the entire trip, I brought a mat that fits perfectly on the outside of my backpack like a giant water bottle. It adds a bit of extra weight, but is the perfect antidote for stiff muscles and a stressed-out travel mind.

Now having a year of travel without the constraints of full-time work, I can focus on improving my yoga postures and become a yoga teacher after the trip. This is the ideal opportunity to practice and enhance everything I've wanted to be.

The sound of chatter collapses the silence as other women set up their mats with close friends and family. Some wear plain t-shirts and loose-fitting pants like me. Others prove their dedication to yoga with streamlined Lycra tops and unforgiving pants. The serious yogis are sitting with eyes closed in a dreamy state, hair pulled up into a cinnamon bun and a thin layer of skin rippling across their bare midsection. The empty spots on the lawn gradually fill in as class time approaches, and I am more than ready to begin.

Basic, slow movements ease everyone into the exercises, and the familiarity feels comforting. Given all the muscle cramping I've endured these past few weeks, I'm curious to see how much I can handle. But the moves flow easily, and my body instinctively knows what to do: cat-cow, downward dog, warrior I, warrior II, triangle, side angle, and gentle twists on my back. I glimpse at the more advanced students beside me and reach a little further in my poses. I will likely be sore tomorrow, but tonight I'm showing the world what I am capable of.

Any mental or physical tension drifts away, and a sense of joy fills my entire body. Several times I look over at the cityscape just across the river, not quite believing that I am taking a yoga class in beautiful Brisbane, Australia. The entire class then falls quiet while resting in corpse pose, although I feel more alive than I have in weeks.

Following the brief meditation I gently open my eyes, re-acquainting my senses with the surroundings. The trees and grass have a rich softness, the air crisp and clean. I tiptoe to the end of my mat, curling it over with care until it forms a large soft tube. A crowd gathers around the instructor to collect free samples of yogurt, but I take my time, wanting to prolong the warm after-effects of this yoga experience.

I grip my mat tightly from the heavy winds across Goodwill Bridge, and enjoy a clear view of downtown. The Treasury Casino & Hotel glows with colourful lights and a large red bow for the Christmas season.

The uphill walk is surprisingly easy, and I watch Brisbane locals streaming through outdoor malls and filling restaurant patios for dinner. At any other time the crowds and noise would have bothered me, but tonight I feel peaceful and content.

By the time I arrive at the hostel, Dean has already prepared a pasta dinner for us. Enjoying a nice home-cooked meal, I gush about my yoga class at the park. Dean listens to all my stories, smiling back at me with pride.

SYDNEY, AUSTRALIA

It's a short walk from our hostel to the Bayswater Brasserie downtown. A menu at the front entrance shows the selections for the evening, printed on cream linen paper with an English-style font. While waiting for our table to get ready, we order a couple drinks at the bar.

"Finally, a well-made martini," Dean says, admiring the speared trio of olives resting on the edge of the glass.

"Cheers to treating ourselves to fine dining!" I say, and clink my red wine glass to Dean's martini.

We grin with delight, and imagine our friends also indulging their taste buds with expensive cocktails and appetizers. But tonight it's just the two of us – my surprise to Dean for celebrating his 36th birthday.

The staff wave that our table is ready. I weave through the empty tables with Dean right behind me, trying to appear normal even though the alcohol has already made me woozy. The waiter smiles and introduces himself while adjusting my chair, and with his friendly Aussie accent describes the menu specialties for the evening. Dean decides to order the crab, and I choose the native Australian Barramundi fish with a side order of green beans. We also order another round of drinks.

"Did you know that celebrities have eaten here?" I whisper to Dean.

"Oh yeah? Who?"

"Hugh Jackman!"

"Wolverine's been here? That's cool."

It was just two days ago that we saw Mr. Wolverine in person. The world premiere of *Australia* was taking place at Event Cinemas in downtown Sydney, precisely at the time Dean and I were staying in the city. Promised to be in the same dramatic genre as *Gone with the Wind*, the film is a pre-World War II romance in the Australian outback between an English aristocrat and a cattle drover, starring Nicole Kidman and Hugh Jackman. Only invited guests were permitted for the screening, but anyone could watch the parade of celebrities walking the red carpet.

The crowds were cheering and screaming, accompanied by an orchestrated ensemble of clicking cameras. I stretched up tall on my toes to see the action while enthusiastic fans pushed from behind, flailing their arms with notebooks and pens for autographs.

I noticed a warm glow of blonde hair and pale skin approaching our area. On her tall but delicate frame, Nicole wore a white, shimmering beaded dress and smiled to the crowd, keeping a safe distance away from the craziness. Her husband Keith strolled behind her, patiently waiting for Nicole to wave and acknowledge the eager fans.

Then along came Hugh, flattering the mostly female crowd with a hint of outback ruggedness while wearing a polished suit and slicked-back hair. His Aussie drawl made the women scream even more. I held out my hand above the crowd, but too many other star-struck fans also wanted a handshake. Luckily Dean managed to snap a few photos to remember the experience.

It doesn't take long for our meals to arrive. The waiter places the dishes in front of us using a linen napkin folded around the edges. The crab legs sprawl out in all directions, requiring fine motor skills to crack open its hard shell. The Barramundi fish is carefully stacked in the middle of the plate, with sprigs of herbs and lemon slices tucked around the sides – a perfect complement to Dean's morning photo session at the Sydney Fish Market. A small dish of green beans is dressed with sliced almonds sprinkled on top.

"Happy birthday Dean!" I say, making a toast.

"Here's to many more fancy dinners on the trip. And no barbecue chickens tonight!" he says.

It's amazing how high-quality gourmet dinners slip from your memory while travelling backpacker style. Our standard fare of deli cooked chicken or spaghetti are easy to prepare, but lack the punch of spicier dishes that require more ingredients than is possible for us to carry between destinations. To avoid an overload of food during our travels, we always hope that the hostel we've booked has free spices and oils on hand for cooking.

However no hostel-cooked meal comes close to the perfection we're experiencing tonight. Our entrees are absolutely delicious, and we complete the meal with a mango and passion fruit tartlette. The tart slides easily along my tongue, and its sweetness is the perfect companion for my dessert cravings. I even leave the last bite for Dean.

I check my watch, and it's almost 7:30 pm. I wave down the waiter to pay our bill, and do my best to disregard the triple-digit total at the bottom of the receipt. But it's worth it, and how many Canadians can say they've dined in Australia for their birthday?

I'm not the only one with surprises. While I enjoyed a backstage tour of the Sydney Opera House earlier today, Dean had purchased floor-level tickets for the Australian Ballet performance of *Interplay*. Sneaking them into our take-away lunch bag, I reached inside to find two tickets for a glamorous night out. Giddy with delight, my thoughts soon turned to how I could match the glamour with my limited wardrobe.

Once the bill is settled we grab our bags, thank our wonderful waiter, and head outside to catch a taxi.

We arrive at the Sydney Opera House just in time before the curtain lifts up. Famous Aussies Nicole Kidman, Mel Gibson, Cate Blanchett and Geoffrey Rush all began their careers at the Opera House. I try imagining them as budding actors on this grand stage, and the excitement of performing inside this stunning theatre. I then try to imagine myself on stage, twenty years younger with the same confidence and talent, feeling the energy stream through my body at record pace.

We are so close to the stage that we can hear the dancer's pointe shoes squeak on stage. The sequences are a blend of ballet and contemporary styles. I study the scores of leaps and turns sweeping across the wood floor; their bodies moving seamlessly like schools of fish in the ocean. We have difficulty following the abstract storyline, but are too captivated by the choreography to care. After the first performance, the dancers come out for a bow.

We turn to each other and say, "Is that it??"

We look around to see if anyone is leaving. There are a few people getting up, but they're not grabbing their coats and bags. It appears that this is simply an intermission.

Feeling relieved, we walk out to the lobby area. The architect of the Sydney Opera House, Jørn Utzen, insisted that all patrons have a view of the harbour, and we couldn't have asked for anything more beautiful. The Sydney Harbour Bridge arches up into the sky, and gently bows down the other side into downtown, highlighting the river below. We can almost see the entire city from this posh foyer, with its royal purple carpeting and rippling wood walls like the inside of a piano. A few minutes later we are signaled to take our seats for the next performance.

Using a few simple props and long, flowing costumes in vibrant oranges and blues, the dancers leap and play with natural ease. The shimmering fabrics billow across the stage, interweaving like kite tails in the wind. Staccato rhythms stimulate the momentum amidst a fluid, curvaceous sensuality. Every dance movement reciprocates in my own body, as I envision the amount of muscle tension needed to perform all the jumps, turns and ballet lifts. I barely breathe through the entire performance.

The house lights gradually expose the entire theatre, and we take one last look before shuffling out of the row of seats. Stepping outside I am bursting with excitement. I create my own dance sequence on the promenade, imagining myself on stage. Wearing a long cotton skirt and top, with a red hoodie for warmth, I spin around streetlamps with my arms outstretched and toes pointed like a ballerina, breathing in the cool ocean air. I nearly kick off my flip-flops to feel more graceful, and skip the rest of the way across the walkway.

As I enjoy the view of Sydney Harbour, Dean is setting up his tripod to photograph the lighted domes of the Opera House. I catch up to him and admire the bright white shells lifting up to the sky like cat's ears. I follow the shape of each ear, its zigzag pattern inching along the outside curve. Soon we are both ready to return to our regular backpacker life, and begin the walk back to the hostel.

❧ Chapter Three ❧

Koru

We're flying over Tasmania, and all I can see is green. It's a patchwork of olive, avocado and emerald sewn together with streaks of brown and blue. Admiring this natural landscape makes me contemplate the two weeks we'll be spending in Tasmania. Mainland Australia was great, but I want Tasmania to be a much fuller, enriching experience. I want more from our trip than the usual sightseeing excursions posted along the sidewalks. I want to explore the countryside and see remote towns – the real Tasmania.

BICHENO, TASMANIA

The bus ride from Hobart to Bicheno takes approximately three hours. We arrive in the windy ocean side town where the sandy beach runs long and deep, and there are just enough services for locals to reside. I love the simplicity of these outlying towns, free of tourist hype and overpriced souvenirs. A sports store clerk in Hobart had commented to me that the people in Tasmania are more about lifestyle than career choice. I immediately wanted to hug this beautiful land.

Dean and I are staying at Bicheno Backpackers, a cottage-style hostel run by a couple that also loves outdoor adventure and travel. Each cottage has four bedrooms and a shared living room, kitchen and bathroom. Inside our cottage we meet Susan and Janet, newly retired friends from Ontario who are travelling the circumference of Tasmania for one month in their rental hatchback. Wearing comfy traveller clothes with short bobs of blonde and brown hair, the ladies welcome us in a familiar, cheerful Canadian style. We share stories of hostels and favourite destinations, and I quickly admire their adventurous spirit when many people their age are contemplating vacations on luxury cruise boats.

The next day all four of us decide to visit Freycinet National Park and hike an 11 kilometre trail that circles around Wineglass Bay and Hazards Beach, taking five hours to complete. We hitch a ride to the park with our new Canadian friends, in exchange for a home cooked roast dinner for all of us to enjoy after the hike.

I begin the hike with a sense of beginner's enthusiasm, chatting with Susan and Janet while swiftly dodging thick roots and sharp stones jutting through the path. Soon after beginning our journey the hills become steeper and the trails uneven. Climbing up rugged, rocky mountains and carefully tip toeing down steep valleys tests my body's strength and endurance.

Some of the climbs are so long that I don't want to look up. I decide to focus only on the next step, and keep my breathing as steady as possible. Susan's quick pace takes her off into the distance as the rest of us struggle to keep going. I envy her stamina, but during this personal challenge she is also leaving behind her friend. I offer words of encouragement to Janet, who is red-faced and winded, while the three of us clamber up the mountain. Before long the exhaustion becomes too much, and I call to Dean and Janet for a rest break on top of a cliff overlooking the ocean.

While my muscles ease back into a restful state, I look around at the trees gently bowing their heads in the breeze. The stillness of nature releases any built-up tension and stress, allowing my breath to become soft again. I close my eyes, letting the wind sway my body from side to side. After a few deep breaths my eyes flicker open, soaking up the beautiful view.

We continue our journey through the forest and reunite at a beach area on Wineglass Bay. The deep blue water in the distance blends into a delicious aqua green close to shore. Large, powerful waves crash down, tempting us into the cool ocean. Unfortunately nobody remembered to bring their bathing suit, so instead we find a sloped, shady ridge to rest our aching bodies. We sit in a row facing the water, munching on sandwiches and drinking lots of water. Movements are slow and conversations simple.

After a brief sunbathing session we agree that it's time to move on. Everyone slowly stands up and stretches out their stiff bodies. We've completed one third of the hike, so there is plenty more to come.

Even after a short break my body feels surprisingly energetic. I bound up hills and skip over rocks until my legs demand to slow down. Once again the steep ascents become painfully intense, like an advanced yoga class. My ankles are wobbly so I carefully place each step to avoid twists or sprains. Getting an injury would make a painful journey and seriously inconvenience the other hikers. Keeping a positive attitude is paramount in my mind.

In the latter part of the hike there are several lookout points up high on cliffs. The stunning views of the bay make me feel whole again after enduring such a difficult climb. Conversations immediately stop as we admire the wide mountain ranges curving around inlets. The turquoise blue water has a smooth, white sandy border, contrasting with dark green broccoli clusters of trees on land.

Anticipating the end of the hike, we begin looking for signs that indicate the Visitor's Centre, but the path keeps zigzagging through the forest with no signs of human life. I lumber along, tipping my bottle up high for the last few sips, hoping that my aching legs won't surrender and fall off.

Then a sign appears a short distance away that I want to hug with delight: *Visitor's Centre 10 minutes*. I jump up and yell to Dean and Janet, "It's only 10 minutes away! We can do this!" The exasperation in their faces changes to smiles of relief, and our pace quickens during the last kilometre of the hike.

We finally reach the parking lot and see Susan resting on the car hood, taking a big gulp from her water bottle. I crave a glass of lemonade, but settle for any bit of lukewarm water. A posting at the end of the trail rates the hike as "difficult", and we all let out a big sigh. The peeling of layers begins on a new perspective of the beauty of life.

LAUNCESTON, TASMANIA

We have had just about enough of the backpacker lifestyle filled with rigorous hiking, carrying 25lb packs that feel like elephants, and staying in bare bones accommodation. After almost two months of travel it's time to indulge in the finer things in life, so we book a room at Kilmarnock House Bed & Breakfast in the quaint city of Launceston. A once-a-month treat – that is our plan for surviving a yearlong trip around the world.

After two and a half hours on a bumpy bus ride from Bicheno, we haul on our backpacks and navigate the downtown streets. According to the map, the B&B doesn't look too far away, however maps can be deceiving. We begin our journey heading east from the bus station, filling up most of the sidewalk like football players, and peeking inside the stylish boutiques and cafés along the way.

The shops gradually fade away and are replaced with large brick homes and the sweet smell of fresh flowers. However the manicured parkland isn't able to distract my mind from the immense weight pushing down onto my aching shoulders. I can barely wait to peel off my pack, along with the many layers of clothes that were essential in blustery Bicheno.

Up ahead I spot a particularly large estate home, and squint to see if it's our destination. I sigh with relief as we quickly cross the busy road. I feel like Santa Claus trying to run with his sack of toys.

A small sign directs us to the back door where we are welcomed in with a pleasant smile. Elizabeth guides us to the front of the house, where peach coloured walls are brightened with white crown moulding archways, and sunlight streams in through floral stained windows. Paintings with thick, gold frames hang on the walls, and by the entrance sits a vase with fresh flowers.

Originally built in 1905, owners Bruce and Elizabeth Clark purchased the property in 1985, and restored and renovated the home to its original Edwardian style. Each of the ten rooms is furnished with antique furniture that is locally handcrafted. It has all the essential furnishings of a royal night of luxury, and I never felt more out of place than right now.

Elizabeth checks our names in the register, and then guides us up the dark wood staircase to our room. I was expecting the usual stares from our scruffy backpacker appearance, but instead she smiles with awe and wants to know more about our trip. While Dean provides a brief summary of our adventures thus far, I follow from behind.

"Don't knock over anything!" I whisper to Dean.

With each nervous step we skim past paintings with distinguished men wearing the finest Victorian ensemble while out in battle. My palm slides up the smooth, curved railing, which helps me to balance the teetering load on my back.

Our room is the first doorway on the left, and Elizabeth unlocks the cream coloured door. I peek inside, and the entire space has the look of a historical museum.

Pastel colours in every shade fill the room. A floral duvet gently rests atop the swirling brass double bed. Next to the window is a perfectly sized table for reading the morning newspaper, with a set of wingback chairs acting as bookends. To my left is a kitchenette complete with a fridge, sink, microwave, and shelves of glasses and China bowls. I glimpse the private bathroom tucked away in the corner and want to jump for joy. For a few days we can live like "regular" travellers in our new luxurious room. Hopefully Dean can survive with all this frilliness.

My rough exterior feels like a threat to all of this delicate décor. As Elizabeth highlights the room features, I try smoothing back my ponytail and straightening the twists in my t-shirt. Meanwhile Dean's hair looks like it's caught in a windstorm, and a dark circle of sweat is showing up under his armpits.

A wooden blanket chest sits next to the window, which looks like an ideal spot to rest my backpack. I turn around and carefully peel off my pack in an awkward squatting position, making sure to avoid knocking off the picture hanging above. After the pack makes a safe landing, I can almost hear a sigh of relief from Elizabeth.

After a few pleasant exchanges Elizabeth lets us settle in, inviting us to try a sample of port in the sitting room outside our room. Dean's eyebrows peak with interest, and after our morning travel I'm also tempted to give it a try.

Yet our need for rest takes over. We close the door, kick off our hiking shoes and moist socks, and let our feet soak into the warm, soft carpet. Dean dives onto the bed and lets out a giant aaaaaaaaaaaahhh. I join him for an afternoon nap, but first look around at all the antique dishes and artwork displayed in the room. It feels like we've been transported back to a time of kings and princesses, and this is our royal palace. It's a shocking change from our usual plain backpacker rooms, and I could definitely get used to this.

I rest for a brief ten minutes, then get up and start unpacking my bag. I go into our wonderfully clean, spacious bathroom and take a moment to enjoy the luxurious surroundings. My fingers caress the thick, white bath towels folded neatly over the glass-enclosed shower stall, the delicate lace curtains tickling the window frame, and all the freebie soaps, gels and shampoos displayed neatly above the vanity. I unzip my toiletries bag and begin lining up my hairbrush, facial cleanser, moisturizer (it leaked again!), body lotion, toothbrush, and everything else that will fit on the narrow wooden shelves.

Strolling back to the bedroom, Dean has escaped into a deep mid-afternoon nap, so I continue to unpack my clothes and souvenirs. There are only a couple of hangers available, but just enough to de-wrinkle a few t-shirts during our stay. My quick-dry towel can finally take a rest while staying here.

I sift through the "important documents" pack and pull out our research on Launceston. We were able to find activities for both of us, and they couldn't be more of a contrast – Dean is planning to tour a local beer factory, and I will be visiting the spa. However this isn't your typical facial and massage therapy clinic. No, Launceston can do much better than that. This beautiful city has Roman Baths! My muscles are twitching with excitement as I read the advertisement.

Dean's eyes flicker open, and after adjusting to the soft light he stretches his limbs to wake up. He rolls to the side of the bed and suddenly remembers the bottle of port waiting to be poured. Dean offers a glass but I decline, as I'd probably fall asleep in my dinner after our long day. Instead I decide to change into some nicer clothes for our usual orientation walk in the city and find a dinner spot downtown.

The following morning we sample many of the food and drinks stocked in our kitchenette: toast, eggs, ham, cereal, fruit parfaits, orange juice and coffee. China dishes add a touch of royalty as we sit by the window in our wingback chairs. I soon realize that the cleaning staff replenish the breakfast foods on a daily basis. I warn Dean how dangerously tempting this is for backpackers, all the while packing a few snacks for nibbling later in the day.

Dean and I walk downtown together, but then part ways for our planned activities. A few blocks away are bright white roman columns adorning the front of the spa building, making it stand out from the neighbouring businesses. I walk inside and discover large columns decorating the interior as well. The receptionist informs me that due to my early arrival I can enjoy a few minutes in the baths prior to my massage appointment. Yes, I think I'll pamper myself in the baaaaaaaths, thank you very much.

The change rooms appear like most in public pools, except for the tropical floral arrangements, opulent sinks and complimentary spring water. No, those features aren't too common in your average community centre back home.

I change into my swimsuit, stuff my clothes into a locker and head out to the pools.

My first glimpse of the Roman Baths is how I imagined it – soft lighting with stone columns and statues bordering the pool deck, and groups of older ladies with perfectly styled hair gently skimming the surface. A few are dozing away the morning in the bubbling hot tubs.

In the main pool ("Tepidarium"), an instructor yells out instructions to a group of seniors in an aqua fitness class carefully balancing on pool noodles. I circle around the deck and slip in at the shallow end. The soothing warm water caresses my skin, and any nervous, fidgety movements become slow and relaxed.

An older stout woman swims toward me, doing a revised breaststroke to avoid her hair having any contact with the water.

"It's a bit cool today, isn't it?" she says.

"Actually it's my first time here," I say, smiling.

"They don't have the jets on. I paid money to have the jets on."

Her lips tighten together as she treads water in the middle of the pool.

"Maybe they'll put them on after the class," I say.

"Well that's not the point now, is it?"

I smile back at her, wishing she would just relax and enjoy the peaceful surroundings. While treading water, I peek my toes up above the water, wiggling them like a little kid. I hope to always have the curiosity and wonder of a child, rather than a life filled with years of bitterness and entitlement.

After a few minutes she swims away and joins a group of other ladies at the far end of the pool. Judging from their reactions and fervent discussion, they're more sympathetic of her distressing situation.

It's been almost half an hour and my muscles can't possibly be any more relaxed, so I climb out and walk back to the change room. I dry myself off thoroughly and get dressed for the massage treatment.

Waiting for the therapist to greet me in the lobby, I overhear another woman comment to the reception staff.

"The water is freezing cold today."

The receptionist makes a few solid attempts to ease the woman's concerns, but none are taken seriously and she huffs her way out the door.

No, she's probably never been a backpacker.

The massage therapist smiles and invites me into the treatment room. I slip out of my clothes and she begins rubbing my back with big, broad strokes. It feels wonderful to have someone else put their strong muscles to work while my body surrenders in response. I gradually fall deeper into relaxation as she kneads around to my legs, arms, shoulders, neck and head. Each limb is gradually elevated with lightness, and soon the heaviness in my body is completely gone.

When she finishes I whisper to her, "That was heavenly."

FLIGHT TO NEW ZEALAND, VIA MELBOURNE

Our Virgin Blue flight lands according to schedule into Melbourne. We rush through to baggage claim, grab our packs, and swiftly make our way to Terminal 2 to get ready for the next flight to Auckland.

Along the way we fill out the customs declaration card. I hesitate at the question, "What is your usual occupation?" I almost fill in my usual answer of "Office Worker", but then turn to Dean for advice. "Put writer," he replies. *But what if they find out I'm not a professional writer?* I write it down anyway, enjoying the way it looks on the page.

When we arrive at the Qantas check-in desk, the waiting area is mysteriously empty. Out of breath, we hand the agent our tickets and passports. Her face looks puzzled as she scans over our documents, then phones Airline Services, who confirm that our flight is delayed until 3:00 pm. Oh well, it will give us time to eat our lunch and relax in the airport lounge. We stroll through the terminal to scan the take-away options, and decide on a couple cheap sandwiches while making our way to the gate.

As we watch planes come and go on the tarmac, a voice crackles over the speakers announcing that our flight is delayed once again due to electrical problems. In the meantime the airline is handing out free meal vouchers to use during our stay in the airport. We groan and take turns to find something more appetizing for our dinner.

An hour later another announcement informs everyone that passengers will be split into two different flights – one at 6:30 pm and another one at 7:30 pm. They add that the electrical problem is due to a dog chewing through some of the wiring. *What kind of dog would do such a thing? And how did it get out of its cage?*

My body slowly stiffens from hours of sitting, reading, and brewing over the adjusted itinerary. I pace the airport shops, hoping to find interesting reading material to look at. However all I find are the usual magazines filled with celebrity gossip and the headlines, "How to make your life great with these amazing tips!" I gradually stroll back to our camped-out spot with two large bottles of water, and find a quiet spot to begin a yoga routine. After a few stretches I'm bored and lay down on the hard floor looking up at the ceiling.

Dean taps my shoulder and says we should e-mail the hostel to let them know we'll be arriving late. Luckily a few computer terminals are close by and we load up our e-mail account.

"Hey Vicki, there's an e-mail from Bruce," Dean says.

"Really? I can't believe he e-mailed back so soon!" I say.

I had a few questions about writing travel stories and decided to e-mail Canadian wilderness author and photographer Bruce Kirkby, never really expecting this famous adventurer to reply back. I read his e-mail slowly, focusing on every word. The message is cool and laid-back, advising us to remember poignant sayings and make notes of key phrases to add into the story later. Given the active nature of travel, it can be tricky to record every detail in the moment, so I appreciate Bruce's understanding and experience in this field. He also plans to follow our yearlong journey through the *Backpack Adventures* website, and wishes us a "wicked, great trip". I'm starting to feel like a *real* writer now.

I relax back on the floor, giddy with delight. Meanwhile Dean types an email to the hostel staff about our situation, and then spreads himself out on the row of seats like a captive waiting for his release date.

The stale air wicks out any trace of moisture, and I reach over to the plastic bottle for a big gulp of water. Dean is slouched in the lounge chair, his eyes glazing over a novel he's trying to read. When I wiggle his foot he nearly jumps out of his chair.

Our flight finally departs at 8:00 pm, and we arrive in Auckland three hours later. With the time difference, it's about 1:00 am Sunday morning. My eyes are burning, and all I want to do is climb into a warm, soft bed. Instead we must retrieve our giant bags and somehow get to the hostel.

We join the crowd of people waiting by the luggage carousel, however only a few bags manage to make it out alive. Airport staff direct us to the Baggage Service line, where about fifty other passengers from that flight are waiting to fill out forms detailing bag descriptions, value of contents, and accommodation for luggage delivery. I want to scream at the top of my lungs if only my body had the energy. They inform everyone that complimentary taxi rides have been arranged for all passengers who were inconvenienced from the delays. The Travel Gods have finally given us a break tonight.

We arrive at the hostel at 2:30 am, aching to go to bed. With only our carry-on baggage, we retrieve our keys from the hostel mailbox and stumble inside. Our room is everything we hoped for. The bed is luxuriously soft with lots of blankets to keep us warm, and we sink into the mattress with pure pleasure.

Two days later Dean wakes me up to say, "Our luggage has been located. It's in New Zealand, and they'll deliver it by 9:00 am this morning. The flight didn't get in until late last night."

I breathe a sigh of relief, knowing that I won't have to spend another day wearing the same stinky clothes. If it were possible to travel with only carry-on luggage, this never would have happened. *What is the least amount of stuff we can live on?* Then I remind myself that every traveller experiences glitches along the way, and these rough spots usually make the most entertaining stories.

At 10:00 am a taxi pulls into the driveway. Hostel staff sign the necessary forms and we haul our bags up to the room. I've never felt so happy seeing my giant backpack – like an old friend that accidentally wandered off. Finally I can shower, change into clean clothes, brush my hair, and maybe even put some lipstick on!

PLIMMERTON, NEW ZEALAND

To celebrate Christmas Dean and I spend the holidays at a seaside lodge in Plimmerton, a small town on the North Island of New Zealand. Moana Lodge is named after the Maori translation for "sea", which is exactly the view we have outside our double room. Dean is excited that he can set up his tripod in front of the window to take photos of sunset while wearing only a t-shirt and boxers. After eleven years of marriage he still surprises me with his simple pleasures.

Dean stretches out on the bed for a nap, so I decide to take a walk around this home-away-from-home. My first stop is the impeccably clean washroom, with beach-themed toilet seats and painted sunsets on the tiles. On the counter are tiny ceramic lounge chairs to hold toothbrushes and soaps. All it needs are a few pictures of surfers on the walls, and I would take this bathroom home with me.

In the living room sits a dusty rose sectional sofa in front of a large bay window, where a cat is stretched out in the sun. The dining area is decorated with vintage photos of Plimmerton, and a guitar and ukulele hang on the wall.

On Christmas Eve, all guests staying at the Lodge are invited to a communal buffet dinner, and everyone can contribute their favourite dish. With room bookings at full capacity, there is a steady stream of guests from Britain, France, Italy, Germany, Israel, Canada and the United States.

Dean and I hike to the grocery store in town to buy food and supplies, and along the way find a pay phone to call our families. The overly complicated international calling card finally connects us to our parents and siblings to wish them a Merry Christmas. They pass around the phone while Dean and I share the receiver. Hearing their voices is comforting after the roller coaster of emotions we've had the last few months. First are the weather and health updates, the complete schedule for their holidays, and all the projects and stellar grades of my niece and nephew. They also thank us for the Christmas gifts of jewellery, tote bags, scarves, books and other Australia-themed souvenirs that we mailed from Sydney.

Dean then briefly summarizes the highlights of our trip and reassures everyone that we're doing fine after two months of travel. I feel tears building up in my eyes, realizing the vast distance between us and their lives back home. Even though Dean and I are on a trip of a lifetime, I crave the comfort of family and friends in our cozy, decorated home during the holidays. I especially miss my cats, and hope they get lots of toy mice to play with for Christmas. After many well wishes at both ends, we hug and remind each other that we're spending the holidays in a warm, tropical country, as opposed to the snowstorms of southern Ontario.

Returning to the lodge, we unload three full bags of groceries onto the counter. The kitchen is a bustling hub of chopping, mixing and roasting. I'm fascinated by everyone's ease of cooking, like they're performing a choreographed culinary routine. To me the task of meal preparation often feels awkward, with so many possibilities for injuries, on top of trying to synchronize the cooking so all the dishes are finished at the same time. Luckily Dean helps to assemble the grilled root vegetables and ham and tuck them inside the oven.

At 8:00 pm, a multitude of platters are officially presented to everyone on the kitchen island, and we all gaze at the feast of food set out before us: Asian salad, lasagna, ham, grilled veggies, sausages, pumpkin soup, homemade bread and scones, and lots of wine to top it off. There are about thirty people who've arrived at Moana Lodge to enjoy this Christmas dinner. Many of us are budget travelers, and therefore not used to such big meals. We take turns to load up our plates and walk them out to the dining table.

With a multilingual "Cheers!" we savour every mouthful from our piled-high dishes. In between bites we share our previous trip experiences, recommendations of great destinations and dreams for the future. We all have the travel bug, and want to experience as much as possible before settling down back home. This sense of togetherness with other people, especially women, feeds my desire for connection that isn't always possible when travelling with your spouse.

No matter how large the first course I always have room for dessert, and tonight is spectacular. Chocolate-dipped crepes, Christmas cake, and gooey, sweet squares arouse all my senses, along with a rich mulled wine that will likely have me dozing off in an hour. I pick and choose my selections carefully, trying not to overdo the indulgences when every other part of my body is telling me to go for it.

NELSON, NEW ZEALAND

The sweet scent of flowers attracts me to his backyard studio. A picnic table sits underneath an airy canopy, just a few feet from his one-story home, where Dean and I relax until the remaining participants arrive. I'm a little nervous in these kinds of new situations – that I won't understand or be able to achieve the set goal – but doing a creative activity will be a nice change from meandering through the usual art galleries and museums. A few more people trickle over to the table, filling the silence with speculations about the day's class.

After a few minutes German-born instructor Stephan Gilberg greets the small group to his bone carving workshop. He leads us into a small building where his carved creations are displayed high on the walls. Smooth, creamy necklaces have crisscrosses and wave-like designs, with pieces of iridescent shell highlighting the tip. Below the finished pieces are large pieces of raw, pale bone.

In the small workshop space Stephan shows the group a collection of designs from previously made pieces. He encourages everyone to start doodling ideas onto a piece of paper, not worrying about the quality of our drawings or the goofy shapes we might dream up. After some hesitation everyone begins sketching swirls, twists and arcs onto the paper. Dean is drawn to the combined shape of a fishing hook and the curved tail of a whale. Wanting to keep an open mind, but unable to resist my favourites, I decide on a simple spiral pattern. I also remind myself to take plenty of notes in order to write an article about this experience.

The next step is transferring the design onto an actual piece of bone. Originating from the leg of a cow, this type of bone is most similar to ivory without resulting in negative consequences. It feels rough and primitive. I pencil in a basic outline, keeping in mind that the shape does not need to be perfect.

New Zealand bone carving is an art form that was passed down from the Maori people, symbolizing stories and beliefs from previous generations. Prior to carving, the instructor says a Maori prayer that is traditionally made before beginning the process. Immediately this one-day class turns into a beautiful tribute to the indigenous culture, and I feel honoured to be part of it.

Stephan shares with the class that he learned the art of bone carving while traveling, and turned his passion into a full-time profession. He now leads daily workshops for tourists in the summer season, and in the winter months is busy assembling materials and building up a portfolio for corporate clients. I admire his dedication and success, and want to carry that enthusiasm back home with me when doubts about my own abilities start creeping in.

Stephan places the bone into a vice, and I practice carving it with a thin hacksaw. He emphasizes that the more relaxed you are, the better the result. I take a breath, relax my hands, and follow the spiralling curve, trying not to focus on the fact that I'm slicing through a real animal's bone. Once finished, the piece pops out easily, although it's still hard to imagine it becoming anything beautiful.

We use a power sander to even up the edges, and then draw the rest of the design with a pencil. The piece is so small that it's a challenge to handle it with large power tools. Using steady hands, a small drill bit pierces through the bone to create empty spaces. It's like excavating through rock on a much smaller scale, and I pray that I don't accidentally cut through some parts. This is especially tricky in tight corners and small openings.

A small hand-held electric sanding tool helps round the edges, giving it a soft look. Depending on the design some edges may be rounded more than others. Strips of sandpaper and metal files are handed out to smooth any bumps or scratches that occurred in the cutting stages. My spiral pendant is now starting to come alive – an amazing feat given its origin. I show Dean my progress, whose whale design is also showing depth with sculpted tail fins pointing upwards.

The final and most exciting step is polishing. A block of clay-like chalk is applied to the electric sander for creating the polish, and Stephan assists during this process. He adds that polishing by hand can take up to three hours. Once complete, he uses a soft cloth to wipe off any chalky bits leftover from the sander. The shiny finish gives the piece a stunning, professional look.

To create the necklace, Stephan loops black string through the top of the spiral and places it around my neck. He then hands me a customized description of the design according to Maori culture:

Koru (the spiral) symbolizes the unfolding life, permanent growth and new beginning. The shape is inspired by the permanently unfolding branches and leaves of the ferns.@

Reflecting on the story, my fingers follow the smooth circular pattern from the centre point outwards. The spiral's perpetual movement feels like the whirlwind schedule of our trip as we explore new countries, cities and small towns, not wanting to stop until all of our energy has been exhausted. While curiosity begins the momentum, wonderment sustains the motion during our journey.

Somehow I instinctively chose this design based on my own desire for new beginnings and growth; creating a life that builds on my strengths rather than tucking them neatly inside a drawer to save for special occasions. There are so many forms of self-expression and choosing one feels limiting. I want to try them all – write, paint, act, dance, sculpt, sing – anything that provides moments of exploration and play.

In this workshop Stephan has taught me the importance of believing in myself and having faith in the creative process, especially in the raw beginning stages. After all of the carving and polishing, I now have a handcrafted necklace to serve as a continuous reminder of my own artistic abilities. He's also demonstrated how projects that celebrate the beauty and unique qualities of our heritage can have a positive lasting effect on people. I am inspired and in love with the idea of creating an everlasting impression of the way life *can* be through the power of art.

In Maori culture bone carvings are traditionally given as gifts. After wearing the piece for some time, you then pass it on to another person (usually a loved one) to remember you by. I turn around to Dean and smile.

FRANZ JOSEF, NEW ZEALAND

"How cold do you think it will be?" I ask Dean.

"I'd wear lots of layers just in case," he says.

With that in mind I pull out short and long-sleeved t-shirts, an arctic fleece sweater, long johns, jogging pants and a jacket. Bundled up like a toddler ready for the first snowfall, I take one last trip to the bathroom. I pray my bladder is strong enough to withstand the eight-hour trek up the steep ice glaciers – a true test of willpower. I certainly wasn't going to use a baggie for bathroom breaks, as advised by the young woman at the tour guide office. Not exactly a lot of privacy on an ice-covered mountain either. Once finished in the bathroom, I slather sunscreen on my face and meet Dean downstairs in the hostel kitchen to pack our lunch.

Only a few other people are sitting in the dining area having an early morning breakfast. We gather up two small tins of tuna, mini carrots, apples and protein bars from the giant fridge. I fill up our bottles at the sink, and stuff the food and water into Dean's backpack.

After a quick bite of cereal we walk over to the Franz Josef Glacier Guides office. It's a peaceful morning in this small town, which mainly serves tourists seeking wilderness adventure tours. We hadn't originally planned to come here, but after visiting numerous museums and other cultural attractions, Dean and I were craving a change of scenery. Plus endless comments from other travellers encouraged us to spend more time in the rugged parts of New Zealand, even if it's a few extra bus rides to get there.

Upon arrival we're provided with wool socks, hat and mitts, waterproof boots, and a cloth bag with crampons for ice hiking. This is serious business, and with all our gear we feel like hard-core trampers about to hike across the continent. It's a few minutes until loading time, and I notice a sign for washrooms. I take full advantage of this toilet opportunity while Dean patiently waits for me in the foyer, learning more about the famous glacier.

Franz Josef Glacier is approximately 7000 years old, and one of the few remaining ice glaciers left in the world. Today it's a remnant of a much older and larger glacier that originally extended out to the ocean. In 1863 geologist and explorer Julius von Haast named Franz Josef Glacier after the Emperor of the Austro-Hungarian Empire.

We load into the large tour bus like coal miners off to work. The bus drives down a gravel road with a dull view, and little evidence of what we're about to experience. We pull into a small parking lot where everyone unloads and double-checks their list of gear to take with them.

The thick forest hides any sign of a giant mountain standing behind. Dark green moss covers leaning tree limbs and the sides of cliffs, making it feel like a miniature rainforest. Water trickles down between slippery rocks, and then cascades into a thick waterfall. The tour guides lead us along a well-used dirt path, which requires some tricky maneuvering to get up and around pointy rocks and steep hills. My right quad muscle becomes strained with the difficult climb, creating tension in my left leg from the extra load. This isn't good, it's just the first part of the hike. I try not to think about it and continue on with the group.

Relief comes when we approach a clearing; a huge bed of rocks covers the ground like a volcanic spill. At first it looks like an easy flatland hike, but I quickly learn to approach each step with caution. Crevices and spiky surfaces test my patience and coordination, and every few minutes I look up to judge how much farther to the mountain.

At the base of the glacier we divide into five groups. Participants choose a group based on their endurance levels – one being the most difficult, and five the most leisurely. Dean and I choose group four to enjoy the sights a little longer and take a few photos. We walk over to our tour guide, Troy, who's sporting a ball cap and red fleece sweater, the sleeves pushed up to his elbows. The rest of us are dressed for an arctic snowstorm.

Troy shows us how to attach the crampons onto our hiking boots. They look like weapons now, but on the glacier will act like cat claws piercing into the ice. He asks if anyone is nervous about the hike. I slowly reach up my hand and reply, "A little, but mostly because I'm uncoordinated." Troy laughs, "Well at least you're honest about it." With a smile of encouragement, he directs me to the front of the group where he can help if needed.

The first part of the hike involves walking over stones and rocks, and the metal spikes from our crampons scratch and scrape the surface. Once we reach the snow and ice I let out a sigh. We walk up steep hills, down valleys and through narrow pathways between large chunks of ice. Along our journey Troy evens out the icy steps with his oversized pick axe, making it easier to walk up and down. It doesn't take long before the steps feel like a cruel

Stairmaster routine. For extreme vertical climbs, the guides install large spikes into the ice, attached with ropes to grab onto for support.

We approach several blue caverns that are perfect for crawling into, and people line up to take photos. The caves were naturally formed from the movement of water and ice over time. I imagine being inside a barrel wave, and slide my hands along the sides on my way out.

The path gradually thins out to a mere suggestion, and walls of pale blue ice tower over us. We hobble sideways in unison between a slivered opening, hoping that nobody gets stuck halfway or has a claustrophobic attack. Given all the twists and turns along the hike, we are impressed how well Troy can navigate his way through this icy maze.

We finally reach the top of a mountain and break for lunch. The group disperses to find private spots along the rocky patch. In the distance is a thin waterfall cascading down the side of a mossy-covered mountain, and below are rough, choppy waves frozen in time. The contrasting landscape makes no sense, as if Mother Nature suddenly became confused over this section of New Zealand.

Dean opens up his backpack and hands me the tins of tuna – but no spoons. Using some ingenuity, we manage to carefully scoop the tuna onto the easy-open lids and spoon it into our mouths without slicing our tongues off. I look around and hope that no one is watching. We also munch on carrots, and leave the rest of the snacks just in case we need more energy later.

After lunch we continue the journey, and layers of hats and mitts are gradually removed from our warm bodies. We're now accustomed to all the icy steps, cramped tunnels and uneven paths that come our way. Before long we reach the top point of the hike, and are completely surrounded by ice and snow in varying degrees of frosty whiteness. Digital cameras click away as I breathe in this moment, feeling like I climbed a miniature Mount Everest.

When everyone is ready, Troy leads the group down the mountain, zigzagging through the peaks of ice. Initially the hike doesn't seem too difficult, but my energy level slowly begins to drain. Approaching the halfway mark I'm close to burnout, and my legs wobble like jelly. Although there are a few bumps and trips along the way, luckily I avoid a harsh fall.

By 4:15 pm we take the last few steps to the mountain base. Troy shakes each participant's hand as we descend, congratulating us on a job well done. *Now I feel like a real adventurer, like those extreme mountain climbers in the travel posters back home.*

We take a much-needed rest on the boulders and remove our crampons. My flat-soled hiking shoes feel light yet strange after getting used to the piercing grip of the crampons, the kind of footwear that would definitely come in handy after an ice storm back home.

Like a slow return to civilization, we backtrack our hike along the thick, rocky riverbed. The exhausting hour-long walk is making me impatient and grumpy. We see other people trekking along the rocks looking fresh and awake; the rest of us are worn-out souls returning from battle. By the time Dean and I finish, most of the group is already in the parking lot chatting with each other. We file onto the tour bus and slump down in our seats. I don't say a word on the ride back. Tears stream down my wind burned cheeks, the only part of my body that hasn't been depleted of energy. Dean looks at me with a soft smile, trying to cheer me up while a young guy behind us remarks, "I don't even think I'll drink tonight."

Dean laughs and says, "You know the hike was tough if a young male is willing to give up drinking." I can't help but giggle the rest of the way back.

～

❧ Chapter Four ❧

The Canuck Tuk

I lean over to Dean on the plane and whisper, "We're not in New Zealand anymore!"

Dean grins as we look out the rounded window for signs of land. Hong Kong is minutes away, where we'll transfer to another flight into Bangkok. The anticipation of seeing a completely different culture brings tingles to my fingertips. We loved experiencing the diverse landscapes and aboriginal art in Australia and New Zealand, but after several weeks the similarities of our lifestyle back home created sluggishness in our day-to-day activities. We're both ready for more challenge, and can't wait to explore this fascinating part of the world.

BANGKOK, THAILAND

I stand before a huge breakfast buffet at The Royal Hotel in Bangkok. Heaps of pancakes and French toast fill large metal pans, accompanied by sticky jars of syrups and jams. Beside the tempting hotcakes are three different kinds of eggs, ham and wieners. The middle tables have traditional Asian dishes of rice, stir-fried veggies, salads, battered fish with sauce, and other meat and vegetable combinations. Off to the side are boxes of Corn Flakes, milk, juice, coffee and tea.

However it's the large fruit platters that catch my attention. Tropical half-moon slices of pineapple and watermelon glisten in the morning sun. I desperately want to fill my plate, but must resist the urge. I need to remember the advice from the doctor in New Zealand: "Stay away from fresh fruit and uncooked vegetables, unpasteurized milk and shellfish. And definitely don't drink the tap water!" he said.

Although our original intention for visiting the suburban Queenstown medical clinic was to obtain a doctor's note for a prescription of malaria pills, the conversation soon developed into a warning about the dangers of travelling to places like Southeast Asia. He offered us a complete list of items to be wary of, as well as horror stories about the fruit being injected with unsafe water and other cautionary tales. Reading over his notes, I wondered what on earth we'd eat.

Scanning the entire dining room, I make mental notes of which foods are safe and which ones are off-limits. Watching the other guests lining up to fill their plates with traditional Western breakfast options, I notice that few people are sampling the Asian dishes. Pancakes it is. Besides, I've been craving pancakes for a few weeks now. I just didn't think I would be eating them in Bangkok.

I make a gooey, syrupy island of pancakes stacked three deep, spilling onto a small mound of scrambled eggs. I find an empty table in a quiet corner of the room, and Dean joins me with his selection of eggs, ham, pancakes, and toast. While devouring the sweet goodness, we watch other tourists fill their plates with slices of fruit.

"Remember what the doctor said? Unless that fruit is actually safe to eat, those people are really going to regret that decision later," I say to Dean.

"Yeah, let's give it a day or two before we try it, just to make sure," Dean says.

We finish breakfast with a flourish, feeling our stomachs expand in an effort to digest all the heavy, greasy food we've just consumed. After a few minutes we walk around the buffet selections one more time. I check the milk container sitting beside the cereal. It's clearly marked with the UHT code, giving it a thumb's up for food safety. I breathe a sigh of relief that there's a lighter, healthier option for breakfast tomorrow morning.

@

When a country's climate rotates between "hot" and "hotter", there is no need for enclosed, winterized vehicles. Filling the circular driveway at The Royal Hotel are rows of tuk-tuks – an open-air carriage attached to a powerful scooter in front – ready to escort travellers to their favourite sightseeing attractions. Dean asks one of the drivers to take us to the Jim Thompson House museum for an afternoon tour. He nods his head and smiles, so we climb inside the carriage, excited about our first official ride.

Our driver expertly circles around the multi-lane Boulevard and heads into the narrow downtown streets. There are lane markings on the road, however cars, tuk-

tuks, scooters, buses and wagon-like structures all seem to fuse together into a mob of speeding chaos. We whip by small shops that appear on the edge of abandonment. Dingy grey apartment buildings match the overcast sky, and a tangle of hydro lines drape along the side. The stale heat and smog has suctioned the life out of everything, but luckily a cool wind refreshes our face during the ride.

After a lengthy ride across town we're feeling the effects of heavy air in our lungs. The driver turns left onto a narrow laneway, just past the National Stadium, and lets us out. Dean pays the driver while I look down the laneway. Vendors in makeshift stalls are selling cheap souvenirs, snacks and beverages from a pop fridge. Some are preparing food for those who want to stop for lunch. There is barely enough room to walk as we dodge between parked cars along the side and those driving on the two-lane roadway.

A few feet away we start to see more greenery than dull concrete. A burgundy wood building peaks through the bushes, elevated up high with a tall, pointed roof. Stepping into the park area we're instantly transported into a tropical sanctuary filled with mature trees and palms bowing down to welcome us. Large potted plants and ferns soften any remaining thoughts of man-made materials outside the grounds. And more importantly they provide much-needed shade from the oppressing heat and humidity. I take a deep breath of the sweet scents surrounding us.

We are greeted with smiles and prayer bows from two young women at the entrance. An English-speaking guide leads us through richly decorated rooms while providing a detailed history of the home. I pull out my notebook and record as many interesting facts as possible, trying to stay focused around all the stunning décor and architecture.

Six traditional houses made of teak wood are combined to form the home, which was designed and decorated by the American-born Jim Thompson, a practicing architect prior to World War II. After serving in the war he decided to find permanent residence in Bangkok, where he devoted himself to reviving the Thai silk industry as a designer and colourist. He used his expertise in architecture to create an authentic and beautiful Thai-style home, which he moved into during the late 1950s.

The home is filled with an opulent blend of Buddhist stone sculptures, intricately carved Teak wood tables and cabinets, blue and white ceramic pots in delicate floral patterns, vibrant silk pillows and traditional wall hangings. At each doorway we must step over a raised wood panel, which according to Buddhist philosophy keeps out evil spirits (and safeguards babies from leaving a room). All the rooms are decorated with love and respect for Thai culture and traditions.

The tour guide leads us back to the landscaped garden area, and she encourages us to visit the Thai silk store and art gallery conveniently located on the grounds. But before shopping I breathe in the fresh moist air of this tropical paradise. I walk around in a heavenly daze, trying to imagine how much money would be needed to replicate this back home – probably a bit more than our savings account.

I wander over to an open-air café tucked behind the main building, and wave Dean over to join me. I look down from the platform and see bright orange coy fish swimming freely in a large pond. Lily pads dance on the surface, and rising up out of the water are bouquets of palm leaves. We find a corner table next to the pond and request a pot of herbal tea to share.

Dean shares a slideshow of pictures he's taken so far, laughing at the contrast between our tuk-tuk ride through smoggy downtown and the jungle paradise we're in right now. I don't want to leave this place, but feel grateful that Dean's photos have captured the beautiful scenery for us to enjoy later.

The waitress brings over the pot of tea, which blends perfectly with the tranquil scenery. We sip slowly, imagining what it would be like to collect exotic pieces of furniture and artwork, coordinated so well with the home's architecture and landscaping. I then dream about our future home – discarding all the plain, Allen-key built furniture and replacing it with one-of-a-kind antiques in deep red and brown tones, accented with swirled carvings and edges. Toronto must have neighbourhoods with stores that specialize in antique-furniture-for-couples-on-a-budget. I just haven't found them yet. However I could start with a few small items like wall hangings and cushions, the kinds of textiles that can only be found in Eastern countries like Thailand.

Before leaving we make one more stop at the Thai silk shop. Distinguished ladies visiting the museum stroll up and down the aisles, pointing out which pieces they want to buy to their husbands standing idly by. Vibrant colours and patterns fill the shelves, and I'm nervous to touch anything with my rough hands. I linger over the neatly folded pillow covers and scarves as long as possible before turning over the price tags.

@

Dean checks the clock, and it's time to get up. It feels like the middle of the night, and unfortunately our alarm didn't go off properly. I move in slow motion trying to get all of my stuff ready. Dean scurries around gathering up his camera equipment and our laundry hanging in the window to dry. We stuff the packs to their maximum, filling outside pockets with used socks, water bottles and whatever else will fit. My yoga mat still sits in its bag, unopened since New Zealand.

Sitting on the edge of the bed, I slip my arms through the padded straps and pull down hard to tighten them. I brace my legs for the added weight and stand up. Dean has a heavier load with an additional camera bag (filled with two cameras, lenses and all the necessary attachments) resting on his chest. We lumber out of the room and down the stairs in a rush to the van waiting out front.

Today we start a ten-day trek through Cambodia with an organized tour group. Going through the itinerary at last night's introductory meeting, the change of pace will be challenging for us. We've become accustomed to more relaxed and flexible travel times, setting our own schedule throughout the trip. But now we must follow the directions of our Canadian tour leaders, Sikai and Scott, who dictate the amount of time at each destination before the next bus ride.

The other challenge will be spending long hours with a dozen other people we just met. It feels like the first day of school, and groups have already formed bringing together the loud, chatty kids, the intellectuals, and the quiet introverts. I put on my best performance to be accepted by all of them.

Everyone else is already sitting in their assigned seats. Luckily Sikai doesn't get too ruffled about strict departure times, and we load into van #1 for the half-day ride into Cambodia. Sikai's Zen-like attitude was likely developed from his recent training to be a Buddhist monk, which he still needs to complete. With a shaved head and loose clothes overtop a seemingly malnourished frame he appears like a "mini monk" – a nickname that Dean and I create just between the two of us.

Four other travellers, plus Scott and the driver, join us on the long journey. Having recently finished school and living in Thailand, Scott is attempting his first trip as a tour leader in training. He's trying his best to appear cool and knowledgeable despite his visible jitters. Fellow Canadians John and Carol are pleasant and outgoing, as well as Louise from Manchester, England. Louise's roommate sits quietly in the back barely acknowledging the other passengers. To pass the time we try a variety of word games, filled with a good dose of humour, before settling into a sleepy gaze out the windows.

The van makes a pit stop at a gas station and variety store along the highway, and I welcome the opportunity to use the facilities. However I soon discover the awkward nature of squatter toilets, and the tricky balancing act of aiming for a shallow porcelain bowl down on the dirty floor with a drain in the middle. Treads are moulded on either side of the bowl to stand on, the only noticeable feature for avoiding slips during this painful process. Next to me is a plastic bucket filled with water and a large scoop floating on top – *what is that for??* Thankfully my quads are strong from yoga and carrying a large backpack on the trip, and I only have to do a number one. I squat as far as possible to avoid accidentally peeing on myself.

I leave the stall with a big sigh, wishing that advances in toilet technology had traveled to this part of the world. As an extra precaution I buy toilet paper at the store for future bathroom experiences. I re-join the group, wondering if anyone else had trouble with the toilets.

The group gathers around a picnic table to fill out applications for our Cambodian visas, attaching a small square photo to each form. Once complete, the local driver collects all the paperwork that will later be given to border officials. Everyone then climbs back into the vans to continue our journey towards the Cambodian border.

After two hours of staring at an endless highway we pull into a small community of vendors clustered in long buildings, goods piled up high underneath faded awnings. Scooters skim by rows of pedestrians and cyclists all sharing the narrow road. Men with baggy shirts and sandals pull teetering rickshaws behind them – their carts filled with bags of rice, potatoes, watermelon and kids sitting on top for the ride. A monk walks by a line-up of mannequins wearing hip hugger jeans, some with their zippers halfway down.

We wait at a small food stand while our visas get

processed, seeking refuge from the oppressively hot midday sun. Feeling drained already, we still have another four to five hours to go. Then I look at all the hard working people around us: a woman cooking Cambodian pork sausages over a steaming grill with a hat and scarf to keep cool, school-age boys hauling heavy sacks of potatoes onto metal carts, and a slim older man pulling a towering load of packaged goods down the busy street. I feel embarrassed for my spoiled, Western lifestyle.

Sikai returns and hands out everyone's stamped passports. We now must wait in line to officially depart Thailand on foot, which is long and achingly slow. With heavy backpacks in tow, a few people take them off and balance the overstuffed packs against their hips, allowing their shirts to air-dry from dark patches of sweat. I remind myself that this is all part of the travel experience and to appreciate every moment. These months of travel will slip by fast, and someday we'll be back to our regular lives in Canada with only faint memories of this amazing trip.

We successfully cross over to Cambodia, switching to a bus for the remainder of the trip. We pass by a heartbreaking succession of dirty, makeshift buildings and street beggars hoping to better their lives through tourist dollars. Sikai had warned us of the impoverished conditions we'll encounter along the way, how Pol Pot and the Khmer Rouge regime had stripped citizens of their pride through torture and massive execution, and that many Cambodians are living on less than one American dollar per day. The politics that dictate these horrific lifestyles is often beyond my understanding, and the consequences of such actions leaves me feeling helpless. When I see children with big smiles and outstretched arms holding cans of pop or beaded bracelets, doing anything to make a sale to rich tourists, I'm frustrated that this responsibility is part of their daily lives. *There must be a better way to support these young boys and girls than to buy cheap souvenirs, but how?*

The bus bounces along pot-holed dirt roads, barely slowing down, until the mud smoothes out into a paved highway. Some people pass the time watching an action movie on the small TV terminal, and others chat about their favourite travel experiences or whom they miss back home. I stare out the window at the battered wooden homes lining the highway, with families out front trying to flag us down to support their cause. I want to hug them all.

We pull into Angkor St. Hotel in downtown Siem Reap by late afternoon. With its dusty roads and small businesses, it is a refreshing change from the hectic pace of Bangkok. Dean and I carry our backpacks up to the room and collapse into bed before tonight's dinner call.

SIEM REAP, CAMBODIA

The morning wake-up call jolts us awake at 4:30am, although in my opinion it's still officially nighttime. Barely conscious, Dean and I slide out of bed and somehow manage to pull on our pants without tripping. Luckily I picked out my clothes the night before to avoid rifling through my backpack in the dark.

Shuffling down the hotel staircase my limbs feel numb. The rest of our group is huddled around Scott and Sikai in the lobby listening to instructions. Dean and I are the last ones to arrive, and barely catch the last bit of conversation before it's time to head out.

Four tuk-tuk drivers wait outside to take guests to Angkor Wat, the largest religious monument in the world. Built in the 12th century under the Khmer Empire, Angkor Wat covers 500 acres of land and is considered to be one of the most important archaeological sites in Southeast Asia. We pair up with fellow Canadians John and Carol and our driver for the day, Mambo. As I step into the carriage I say, "We're the Canuck Tuk!" and the laughter helps clear our foggy heads.

Cambodia's daytime weather rarely dips below 80 degrees Fahrenheit, but at night the air is chilly. We chug along at a swift pace through the quiet city streets, the wind whipping our hair in all directions. A thick black void prevents any view of the landscape, forcing our driver to carefully navigate all the curves and bumps of the road. I firmly grip the side of the tuk-tuk as if I'm on a blindfolded roller coaster ride.

Mambo drops us off at the gated entrance, and we join other tired but dedicated tourists in line to buy day passes. Eavesdropping on the customers ahead of us we soon discover that all visitors must have their picture taken for entry. Afterwards we huddle around and laugh at the dull gaze in our photos – much worse than the most embarrassing driver's license ID card.

Scott takes the lead as we stumble our way through the dark towards the large, glassy pond. I try to follow the sound of footsteps along the paved road, hoping that the people in front of me are avoiding any bumps and crevices. I sense a large sculpture just a few feet ahead. The stone bristles against my moist palm, and I stop for a moment to feel the curves of the rock. I overhear other tourists say that we are at the entranceway to Angkor Wat. Now we just need the sun to reveal its beautifully carved features.

I soon realize that I've strayed away from the group. I look around, but it's still too murky to find familiar faces. I feel like a lost child at the fair, and begin walking in all directions past the stony entrance.

A few minutes later I reach a wooden bridge and hear familiar chatter from our group. I skip over and let out a big sigh. Dean also rejoins the group after getting lost, and I squeeze his warm hand into mine. We find a spot to sit on the dewy grass, and listen to mosquitoes buzzing around the pond. I pray that there's enough collective bug repellant in the air from other tourists to avoid us catching a severe case of malaria.

The minutes pass and still no hint of dawn. Just as I start getting restless I notice a faint outline of Angkor Wat in the distance. Like a Polaroid photo, the pond and grassy area gradually come into view. Soon a warm cream-coloured sky begins to emerge with a soft peach outline, and the craggy rocks of the temple become clearer, proudly reaching up high into the sky. Barely a breath can be heard among the captivated crowd.

Scott then asks the group if we'd like to go for breakfast. It seems a little soon, but perhaps the sunrise is finished? We gather up our bags and start walking toward the restaurant, even though other people stay seated watching the sky. As we shuffle along the grassy field, Dean turns around and sees the glowing yellow sun rising up behind Angkor Wat. The golden citrus sky is reflected in the pond, shadowed by a double image of the stone temple. We scramble for our cameras and madly click away before the magic disappears.

PHNOM PENH, CAMBODIA

Tonight feels like date night, Cambodian-style. Just a few days before Valentine's, Dean and I put on our best outfits to celebrate. The tuk-tuk driver picks us up at our hotel and whips along the streets of Phnom Penh. A cool breeze takes the edge off the late afternoon humidity. Each time we've taken a tuk-tuk ride in Thailand and Cambodia it feels like a stylish go-cart race.

The driver pulls up along a quiet neighbourhood street in front of Friends restaurant. The building is bright yellow with a scene of animated characters painted along the bottom. Potted trees and flowers lead guests to the main entrance, creating a welcoming atmosphere compared to the gloomy historical sites we visited earlier today. I then notice another colourful building next door.

The sign out front reads "Friends'N'Stuff", and I can't resist taking a peek inside. I walk slowly around the store admiring the handmade clothing, jewellery, purses, and craft items. Far from the level of a charitable bazaar, the skilled craftsmanship and artistic designs show the ingenuity of these local artists: necklaces and bracelets created from tightly rolled pieces of recycled paper, colourful shoulder bags and wallets made from candy wrappers, and dress tops in a variety of unique patterns. The sales clerk informs me that many of the products are made by parents of children in need who benefit from the various programs run by the Friends organization. *Yes – this is how I can help children in Cambodia!* After circling several times, I decide to purchase a necklace made with small cloth-covered tubes dangling on strings of waxed linen. I immediately try it on with my outfit, feeling grateful that I can help in this small way to change people's lives. After thanking the clerk we head next door for our dinner.

Dean and I are greeted with warm smiles and prayer bows by the staff just outside the restaurant. Vibrant blues and yellows cover the walls, complementing the art displayed around the restaurant. The paintings show an impressive degree of insight and creativity, and we soon discover that students have made all of this artwork. I feel so proud of these young students I've never even met.

A waiter shows us to our table and gently hands us menus with a smile. I already have a good feeling about this place, simply based on the professional décor and focus on local artists. After scanning over the long list of tapas, we decide to order the pumpkin soup; toasted pita with grape tomatoes, hummus and sprigs of basil; fish with tomatoes and mint; and stuffed pasta in a tomato sauce. For a treat I also order a raspberry and vanilla shake.

On our table is a brochure about Friends The Restaurant. This non-profit business is run by former street kids, and is part of the Mith Samlanh Friends program to protect and help youth make improvements in their lives by learning skilled trades. The restaurant and gift shop next door are just one of the projects developed to meet the needs of street children in Cambodia.

There are several steps in the student learning process, and working at Friends is the final phase of their practical training. Once students finish the training they continue their new careers at some of the top hotels and restaurants in Cambodia.

The waiter brings out our drinks and sets them carefully on the table. Each movement is thoughtfully planned out and presented with a smile. The shake is smooth and sweet, the best I've tasted in a long time.

A few minutes later he returns with platters of tapas, all presented with artistic flair. While sharing the dishes Dean and I admire the high quality of cooking from these budding chefs. We scoop up every spoonful, enjoying how each one blends in perfectly with the next. Aside from the local restaurants that Sikai and Scott have taken us on the group tour, Friends has satisfied our desire for a gourmet dinner in an ambiance of colour and beauty. We only wish we had an appetite for dessert.

With a delightful grin on his face our waiter gathers up the empty platters. As Dean pays the bill I circle the restaurant one more time to observe the student artwork. Everyday scenes of their homeland are depicted in large paintings, along with smaller portraits and stunning images of Buddhist figures. Many skill levels are displayed, making it an ideal place for budding artists to showcase their work.

Dean and I also make a donation to Friends for their "Buy a Brick" campaign, which helps fund the Mith Samlanh Centre in Phnom Penh. Once the organization has reached their target our names will appear on one of the bricks. Although we won't see the completed project I'm pleased to help with their worthy cause.

We stroll down to the lakeside park filled with friends and families enjoying the cool outdoor air. The wind whips between masts displaying flags from around the world. Several activities are buzzing with excitement including an 80's-style aerobics class to dance music and a fascinating game of shuttlecocks. Players in this badminton-style game rebound the birdie to the opposite team with their feet. Advanced players are hitting the birdie with amazing ease while balancing on their hands in a donkey kick. Wanting to try this challenging game, Dean buys a shuttlecock from a nearby street vendor. We both agree that with our limited coordination, we need to master the tricky technique back home before embarrassing ourselves in this crowd.

Continuing our walk along the busy streets, I spot a local gallery displaying contemporary art – Asasax Art Gallery.

"Oooooh, let's go inside!" I say to Dean.

The colourful paintings depict statues from Cambodian temples in a refreshingly modern style, reminiscent of Andy Warhol. Creative juices pump through my body, and I ache to grab a paintbrush. Buying art is the next best thing, but unfortunately the print size and prices make it impossible. Luckily they also sell t-shirts with similar designs, so I scoop up a blue one to replace one of my other worn-out backpacker tops.

Our final stop for the evening is meeting our tour group buddies at the Foreign Correspondents Club (FCC). Several decades ago this restaurant was a hotspot for journalists and photographers covering major political stories. Today it's a trendy spot for locals and tourists to hang out. Trying to find the place turns out to be an adventure in itself – flipping through travel guides at a bookstore and asking locals for directions – but is well worth the effort.

Black and white photos depicting the harsh conditions of war and relief aid hang on the walls of the modern restaurant. Dean looks at each one, sparking his ambition to become a photojournalist, a dream he's had since picking up a camera as a teenager. He sits in one of the leather chairs with a backdrop of vintage news stories behind him and smiles for the camera. I've never seen him look sexier than he is right now.

We climb one more flight of stairs to reach the rooftop patio where we spot John, Carol and Louise enjoying a beer overlooking the city streets. We share stories about our evening, and the camaraderie reminds me of the pub back home when we made the decision to travel the world. I then remind myself that we're living our dream right now in the capitol of Cambodia. I put my arm around Dean's waist and hope the magical evening will never end.

❧ Chapter Five ❧
A Traveller's Home

CAIRO, EGYPT

"Well, what did he say?" I ask Dean after he hangs up.

"He's on his way. Hany said his brother looks like a fat oaf," Dean laughs while hauling on his backpack.

The hotel owner has assigned his brother the important task of picking up guests at the airport, and although he's running a little late, I feel grateful that I won't have to explain our destination to an Egyptian taxi driver. We find a spot to rest our packs and I check my watch. It's getting late in the afternoon. *I wonder what Cairo rush hour is like?* I ponder this while tilting my head against the wall, desperately wanting to lie down on a comfy bed and relax the rest of the day.

Half an hour later Dean notices a large man barreling up the steps to the front doors. He's sporting a plain cable-knit sweater and baggy jeans, and has glazed-over eyes like a lost boy. That must be him.

"You going to Juliana Hotel?" he asks.

"Yes, I just called Hany. I'm Dean, and this is my wife Vicki."

He nods and waves his arm to follow him out to the airport parking lot, where he loads our packs into the back of his old, compact car. He quickly sweeps away some leftover papers and wrappers before we climb inside, and then crouches down into the front seat. The car grumbles to a start, and I press my hands against the seat in anticipation of a bumpy ride.

Once we clear airport grounds the traffic bulges into a honking, exhaust-fumed parking lot. Our driver bangs the steering wheel with his palm and lets out a tired sigh. "Traffic in Cairo, always busy," he mutters. The car stops and starts down this packed roadway, with drivers yelling and swinging their arms out windows.

Lining the streets are sand-coloured apartment buildings pressed together with clothes strung across balconies. Downtown streets have a mix of Arabic and English billboards advertising a variety of recognizable brands. While I'm curious about visiting historical sites like the Egyptian Museum and Pyramids, I'm also looking forward to modern conveniences, crossing my fingers that squatter toilets are now behind me.

It takes more than an hour to arrive at the hotel. Our driver squeezes through narrow streets where cars are double and triple parked, with a few wheels sharing part of the crumbling sidewalk. He pulls up in front of a tall, plain building. Uncurling himself out of the front seat, our driver unloads all of our bags and guides us into the building. We squeeze into a cramped elevator that chugs all the way up to the top floor. When the door opens I spot a sign for Juliana Hotel. I let out a long sigh.

Hany greets us with a big smile. He has the same dark hairstyle and oval face as his brother, but is in slightly better shape and fluent in English. Just behind him on the warm, cream-coloured walls are woven rugs with camels and desert sunsets. I immediately feel at home and want to snuggle up on the bed. But before we settle in Hany informs us that we'll be staying at a nearby hotel for one night due to an accidental overbooking. "It's just down the street, at my good friend's hotel," he says. We're then quickly escorted out and back into the car.

The Palace Garden Hotel is multiple blocks away but in the same neighbourhood. The exterior is a bit worn, but the ground-floor lobby looks bright and inviting. A doorman greets us inside, and within a few minutes we're guided down the hallway to our room.

Dust and mould fill the air in this cold, lifeless room. Dark blue polyester drapes hang from a bent curtain rod and smudge marks stain the pale walls. The bathroom probably lost its shine thirty years ago. I decide to wait until tomorrow to take a much-needed shower, and sit on the edge of the bed frozen with tension. I imagine awful creatures crawling around at night while shivering under thin sheets and stinky pillows.

Desperately wanting to escape, we discuss our accommodation options. However without phones or a basic understanding of the downtown streets we have no idea where to begin looking. I crave warmth and comfort, and feelings of homesickness churn in my stomach. Dean starts pacing the floor, and says we should try to find some dinner before it gets too dark. *Yes, let's get the heck out of here.*

Down the street is a convenience store, so we buy a few basic items like peanut butter, bottled water and packs of Nutella. These will at least get us through the day until we can find a supermarket with more food options other than late-night snacks.

We navigate our way through the twisty streets, passing by several Embassy buildings with guards standing out front. With no crosswalks or intersections in sight, we hold hands and dash across the speeding traffic to the Nile River walkway.

Tourist cruise boats glide down the river with smaller boats chugging along beside. The water is comforting, and my pace becomes slower and more relaxed. I feel a gentle tug on my arm from Dean, who reminds me to look for good places to eat, but all I can see are skyscraper hotels and government offices. We turn east from the river, hoping to find some local cafés or restaurants to choose from. There's nothing on the next street so we try another, and another and another, taking us further away from familiar territory. The entire neighbourhood appears to be filled with questionable street food and spooky back alley eateries.

Before long the cobalt blue sky turns to black. Cars whip by us as I try to read the map with diminished light. Nothing makes sense. On a street corner Dean stops and throws his arms up in defeat. *Oh no, now I have to try and figure this out for both of us.* Panic invades my entire body. I look around, trying my best to navigate in the dark, but the lack of street signs makes it nearly impossible. I then realize how much more painful this must be for Dean. Egypt was the country he was most excited to explore, and to have it begin so badly must be crushing his soul.

A couple of young Muslim women passing by offer to help, but they also don't know the city well enough, or the English language, to guide us back to the hotel. My head is spinning with fear and frustration looking for any sign of direction. My breathing is barely noticeable, tightly controlled from the depths of my gut. *We're going to be stuck on the dirty streets of Cairo all night with no one to help us, never to be found again.*

The Travel Gods must have heard my plea for help. In the distance is a round glowing light at the top of a towering hotel. On the map it shows the same shape, so from that reference point I'm able to pinpoint our location. We're alarmingly further than expected, but now we can weave our way through the streets with relative ease.

It takes us more than an hour to return to the Palace Garden Hotel. Although I'm grateful to be back, the creepy décor shifts the tension in my stomach from terror to dread. Still craving a tasty, wholesome meal, we ease off hunger pangs with leftover buns, peanut butter, and one of the emergency protein bars we bought in New Zealand. We gulp it down like it's the last few pieces of food we'll ever eat.

Within a few minutes I'm already sleepy from the lingering jet lag. While Dean cleans up our snack food table I do a quick brush and flush. We switch off the overhead light and climb into bed, trying to ignore any shadows that form in this unfamiliar room. Wearing our warmest pajamas, we both huddle under the covers and pray that we'll sleep through most of the night.

Dean and I wake up the next morning, still cold from the night before. We pull on our jeans and hoodies, not really worrying about how we look or the stale odour in our clothes. As I pack up my stuff, Dean looks over at me.

"What's the matter? Are you okay?" he asks.

"Oh, I just want to kill someone right now," I reply, whipping my clothes into the pack.

Dean gives me a hug and says, "Don't worry, if things don't work out we'll bail and go somewhere else. I promise. I've been feeling homesick too."

I hug Dean back, feeling a mix of sadness and gratitude for such an understanding husband.

Once everything is stuffed in tight, including my lonely yoga mat still bound to the outside of my backpack, we haul our bags out of the room and into the rickety elevator. The metal door slides closed and chugs us down to the first floor, where we wait for Hany's brother to pick us up once again.

A few minutes later he rushes into the lobby and immediately starts gathering up our bags and loading them in the car. We climb into the back seat and enjoy a quiet ride through the Garden City district. Gazing at the mature trees and flowerbeds, I try to empty my mind from our first day in Cairo.

Back at Juliana Hotel Hany greets us with a smile, apologizing for the reservation mix-up. I'm bristling with resentment, but just stand there while Dean acts as a gracious guest. He shows us to our room, and the cozy bed I was craving last night is now in front of me. A red comforter is neatly folded over the double size bed with a thick blanket draped across the end. Matching drapes are pulled to either side of a large window, providing a warm, sunny glow throughout the room. We drop our bags on the floor and collapse with exhaustion.

@

The next day Dean and I visit the Egyptian Museum, passing through two metal detectors before arriving at the admissions booth. The crowd of people makes it difficult to see inside, but after clearing the entrance we are transported into the world of Egyptian royalty.

My Art History class has come alive. No longer do I need to imagine the real life artwork in my coffee table-sized textbooks, or from the stack of flashcards I made to study for the final exam. The actual stone statues are right in front of me. Twice the size of any human, Kings and Queens from ancient Egypt proudly wear wrap-around skirts and sheath dresses on trim, muscular bodies. Their dream-like eyes look past me as they sit on their thrones unaffected by the bulge of tourists gathered around.

Dean and I walk slowly around the museum tilting our heads up to the creamy white curved archways and stone columns separating each of the exhibit rooms. The dry, dusty air creates a soft haze throughout the building. Coffins and cabinets are evenly spaced between statues like chess pieces, and in front of the artifacts are typewritten descriptions, adding a touch of old-fashioned charm for history enthusiasts.

I've never really had an interest in digging through mounds of dirt to search for bits of clay pots or skeleton parts from centuries ago, but after seeing the museum labels I'm curious about what it was like in the early 1900s when the museum was built in Tahrir Square. I envision teams of people organizing displays of ancient coins and jewellery, using manual typewriters to compose the labels, and refurbishing the ancient treasures to their original beauty. *Maybe it would be cool to live in a time of great exploration and discovery like Indiana Jones.* I catch up with Dean, who's studying a cabinet of curiosities, and allow my mind to continue in this make-believe world.

At the far end of the museum is King Tutankhamun, the famous Egyptian pharaoh of the 18th dynasty, attracting the most visitors with his gold funerary mask and coffin highlighting the entire room. I study all the details of the mask – penetrating eyes outlined in thick blue that stretch to the sides of his face, a striped headdress in gold and vibrant blue, a long, interwoven beard hanging just below his chin – and realize that this is probably the oldest, most significant piece of history I will ever experience up close. I take one last look and then continue my way around the room to see the same golden, jewelled features in his throne chair and personal adornments. All of this for a young man who hadn't yet reached his twenties.

By noon we're feeling hungry for lunch, so rather than risk trying to find a local eatery, we head straight for the Nile Hotel restaurant next door. As soon as we walk in we see a sign for a salad bar, and immediately request a table for two. The huge selection of options circling around the buffet causes our mouths to gape open in glee, and I almost start crying. It's the best food we've seen for days.

We load up our plates with endless salad items including hummus, veggies, rolls, soup and dessert tarts. I want to take a scoop of everything and pack the leftovers to store in our hotel room, but out of dignity keep the portion sizes to a small Thanksgiving-sized platter.

At the first bite we melt with happiness. Our diet of white bread, peanut butter, protein bars and bottled water has only created a bulk feeling in my stomach, with little satisfaction or stamina to keep us going. We really need fruit and vegetables to feel healthy again. I've almost forgotten the taste of fresh food in a rainbow of colours, and the way it delights all of my senses. I glance over at the waiters, who keep smirking at us gobbling up the food, and wonder if other starving backpackers have dined at this restaurant out of desperation.

Our bellies expand two pant sizes from the large meal. I try one more dessert, just because it's staring me in the face with its sugary goodness, and want to stretch out on a soft, luxurious bed for an afternoon nap.

ALEXANDRIA, EGYPT

For our second week in Egypt we decide to take the train to Alexandria for a few days getaway from clogged Cairo. During our journey Dean shows me tourist brochures with photos of their beautiful waterfront curving around the tropical blue Mediterranean Sea. I can't wait to be close to the ocean again.

The train trip is just over two hours, however when we approach Alexandria I don't see any signs of the luxury city I was expecting. Instead it's the same dirty, half-built concrete buildings we saw in Cairo. As we step off the train I cross my fingers that the downtown area is more developed and attractive.

The taxi ride to Union Hotel passes by buildings with laundry hanging off window ledges and lots of tiny convenient stores selling snack foods. The hotel is right along the coastline, which could be promising, but turns out to be another old building with aging décor. With barely a smile, the front desk clerk looks up our reservation and asks us which room type we want: big or small bed. We choose the big bed to treat ourselves, and another staff person shows us to our room. As we turn down the hallway I realize that we won't have a seaside view. In fact we have a clear view of the rickety building next door with their clothes hanging over the side. It must be laundry day in Alexandria.

The room has a cold chill in the air, which will only get colder as night approaches. They don't seem to have any heaters in Egypt, so you need to huddle under the blankets to stay warm. The furniture looks like it hasn't moved since the 1950s. A thin, dark blue comforter brightens up the pale room, matching the heavy drapes on the window. I peek inside the bathroom with crossed fingers. The pale tub has permanent stains around the sides, and the sink taps desperately need to be replaced. The most disturbing feature is a strange wire sticking up inside the toilet bowl, close enough to make my butt cringe. *When is the next flight to London?*

Dumping our packs on the bed, we leave our icky room behind to explore the city streets for some good local cuisine. Just like Cairo though, it becomes a challenging task. We do find a cluster of shops selling men's suits, colourful women's dresses and scarves, and makeshift stores with shoes hanging all over the walls. Down another street are the familiar fast food chains of KFC and McDonald's. It's tempting, but even in desperate situations I can't bring myself to eat this mass-produced processed food.

Luckily we discover a restaurant that's close to Union Hotel where they serve regular meals. Dean orders a pizza and I get a chicken salad, trying to load up on vegetables whenever possible. Observing the other locals in their pretty scarves, skirts and blouses, I feel out of place in my canvas pants and sweater. However once our meals are served I ignore everything and devour the plate of food.

The next day for lunch I peel open a packet of peanut butter, using a plastic knife to spread it over a slice of stale pita bread. I look over at Dean, who's still napping on the bed. My taste buds are bored with the nutty paste, but I manage to chew it down anyway.

This isn't a way to live. Why are we doing this to ourselves? We gave up our jobs, our house, our life in Toronto – for this. We're now living in a low-budget hotel room and eating scraps of food because we can't find a decent supermarket to get groceries in this goddamn country. My digestion hasn't been normal for weeks. I desperately want to be somewhere that I can connect with. I want to go home.

Waking up groggy, Dean adjusts his eyes to the bright sun peeking around the blue polyester drapes. I gulp down the last corner of bun and smile at my one true source of comfort, my travel confidante who understands all my quirks and anxieties, good and bad.

I think about all the brave women who travel on their own like independent warriors to the most exotic places, without the need for guidance or support. They easily mingle with locals and fellow travellers, and have enough muscular strength to lift two canoes. My sensitive frame can barely manage all the lugging around, and we've barely reached the halfway mark on our trip.

We escape the hotel and stroll along the coastline, hoping it will brighten our spirits from the stress of travel. The stone pathway is rough, with broken pieces getting in our way. Faded gray buildings blend in with each other. Only the blue sky and ocean waves add any hint of life to this weathered city.

We take a break halfway down the coast, and I perch on top of the stone barrier wall. Dean looks up at me, and all my emotions rise up and fall down in tears. I crumble in front of him, hoping that his soft words will make me whole again. Sadness and guilt fill my exhausted, limp body. I reveal to Dean that if I had the choice, I would get on the next flight to London.

"When was the last time you felt really happy?" Dean asks.

I take a moment to think back, then reply, "The Sydney Opera House."

Dean's face turns from concern to disbelief, so I try my best to explain.

"You see, I'm into theatre and the arts, and the places we've been to didn't really have any of that. I'm so sorry for being this way."

I desperately want to feel inspired. It's getting to the point where I just don't care anymore – the stress of rotten accommodation, trying to find healthy food, getting lost in the city, and not seeing anything of real interest. My motivation for travel has dipped to alarming levels, and most days it's a chore to get through the day.

But all of this feels trivial when I look into Dean's eyes. The caring wife inside me scolds this self-centred attitude. I should be more supportive, especially when Egypt is at the top of Dean's travel wish list. His love of history and ancient civilizations match perfectly with this culture, and I can't let my depression get in the way of his enjoyment.

Dean lifts me down off the ledge and wraps his arms around me. I melt into the curve of his neck, and try to pull myself together. After a few moments we retrace our steps back to the hotel, cupping my hand in his, and freshen up for our evening dinner.

Dean and I follow the curving coastline to reach a restaurant that claims to have the best seafood in the city – The Fish Market. Along the way, dinghy boats paddle by with nets tangled around flopping fish. Some are already on shore, with a line-up of men sorting through the day's catch. Dean stops and reminisces about taking rides as a child in his grandfather's fishing boat in Newfoundland. I smile back at him, enjoying the way he becomes that curious young boy again who loved to be out on the water.

The restaurant is perched up high overlooking the Mediterranean. Although the seaside dining area is already booked, we still get a breathtaking view from our table. Vibrant blue and white linens cover the tables, with carefully placed dishware to match. A waiter immediately brings us menus with a wonderful array of dishes to choose from. He encourages us to try the buffet-style dinner, so we put our trust in him and walk over to the line up of people standing by a large display case.

Enthusiastic servers stand behind the domed counter pointing to the varieties of fish resting on ice. They are accustomed to speedy service, with little time for lengthy explanations or slow decision makers. I choose the standard white fish, and Dean tries a more exotic blend of squishy seafood that makes me wince.

We return to our table and find a dozen bowls spread out on the table: salads, pita bread, beets, a large platter of raw vegetables, and several varieties of hummus dips. We look at each other in disbelief. *Do we have to pay for all of this? Have we been scammed?* I signal the waiter to come over before we start diving into this delicious food.

"Excuse me, we didn't order all of this," I say.

"It is part of meal. You will not be charged extra," he reassures me.

Our eyes light up, and we spoon samples of each dish onto our plate. I devour the beautiful raw vegetables, plunging them into the smooth, swirled hummus. I take a bite of fish and it melts on my tongue. The salads and beets and pita bread all blend together on my full plate. We stuff ourselves until our stomachs swell in joy, and then sit back like kings after a large feast.

There are still lots of vegetables left on the platters, too tempting to leave behind. The waiter generously packs the leftovers into a large cardboard box, enough for at least three more meals. My wish for abundant, healthy food has been granted, and I look forward to happy tummy days again.

ISTANBUL, TURKEY

I love Turkey already. Dean and I rest in the back seat of the comfy Sedan, gazing out the window at the modern highway and skyline in the distance. Traffic flow is controlled with markings on the roads, and drivers change lanes without honking or yelling at each other. Breathing in this country will be much easier too, without a constant billowing haze of exhaust fumes filling the air.

I feel so grateful for this country upgrade that I almost start crying on the way to the hostel. Our airport pick-up was on time, and the driver's clean, modern car feels shocking after riding in tin can vehicles with our bags thrown onto the rooftop. I can't wait to explore the city and enjoy being a tourist again.

@

Downtown Istanbul has invigorated my love for arts and crafts, and I'm instantly drawn to silk pillow covers and metal lanterns with mosaic-patterned glass. At a gift shop near the Grand Bazaar market, I discover beautiful handmade ceramic bowls. All of them are tempting, but I eventually choose a set of teal green bowls, each with their own swirling design. The owner wraps them in paper, and I pray they'll survive the rest of our trip.

I've been dreaming a lot about our future home back in Canada. Just having a place with a private kitchen and bathroom will be a treat. Hostels and hotel rooms are temporary places to store our belongings, but in a home you can grow and create your own beautiful world. I imagine it being a sanctuary with all the amazing artwork we've

110

collected during our travels.

Outside a rug store an older woman is weaving yarn through a loom. We walk over to take a look, and she immediately invites me to sit down on her stool. After a couple demonstrations I loop the coloured wool around the tightly wound threads. We communicate through nodding heads, and she smiles when I finally get it right.

A salesman invites us to "just take a look" at his selection of carpets inside. Rolls and rolls of woven creations line the perimeter of his store, each with a different design and texture. An assistant suddenly appears with two glasses of Turkish tea, encouraging us to enjoy a cup while they show us their full inventory.

Carpets are quickly rolled out and spun around in the air, where they float softly onto the shop floor. We learn about the different weaves and handcrafted quality, and those that "will last for generations". A resident kitty scampers into the store and starts playing on the carpets, distracting me from all the sales pitches. With the kitten as my main focus, the salesman turns his attention to Dean, who can still be lured in for a sale.

After dozens are tossed onto the floor, it's now time to narrow down the favourites. The salesman teaches us the Turkish words Evet ("yes") and Hayir ("no"). At our command, the assistant arranges the carpets into different piles. We finally choose a design that has a mix of traditional and contemporary styles; its diamond pattern in red, black and beige will blend perfectly with the burgundy cushions I found in Cambodia. I am bursting to begin decorating – now we just need an apartment.

BURSA, TURKEY

I yearn for colour and warmth on this grey, drizzling day. The cab drops us off in front of the Karagoz Museum in Bursa, and its Ottoman-style architecture stands out from the surrounding parkland. Detailed carvings of puppet figurines dance around the top of the cream-coloured building, with mosaic scenes of their puppet shows displayed below. We cross the busy road and follow the colourful characters towards the entrance door.

The main floor galleries include a history of Karagoz Puppet Theatre and an exhibition of original puppets from the children's plays they produce. As I examine the displays, I learn that the two main characters are Karagoz and Hacivat, with a supporting cast of other unique characters.

Shadow plays have been around since before the Ottoman Empire, and have grown significantly over the years. Turkey's prestigious International Puppet and Shadow Theater Festival has been organized in Bursa since 1993, attracting famous puppet and shadow theatre artists from around the world. Hosting these festivals not only highlights the artistic quality of Karagoz, but also keeps this art form alive.

Workshops are regularly held at the museum for youth to learn the art of Karagoz puppet making and performance. Coincidentally a workshop is taking place during our visit. Dean takes this golden opportunity to introduce ourselves to the museum staff as a travel writer and photographer from Canada, who graciously allow us to observe the class in progress. I follow Dean into the room, hoping that my smile will mask the feeling of being thrown onto the stage without any rehearsal.

Teenage girls and boys are gathered around a large table filled with colourful paints, cardboard cutouts, and thin pieces of hardened leather. The workshop leader, Nevzat Çiftçi, guides the eager students in this craft-making process. Although Nevzat speaks only in Turkish, a bilingual student helps translate his stories and instructions for creating Karagoz puppets.

The first step is drawing the design onto white cardboard, cutting out any necessary holes, and transferring the figurine onto dried camel leather. Acrylic paints are used for colouring, with white dotted lines to highlight the layers. Each of the limb joints are then pinned together for making action moves like walking or waving their arms. The last step is attaching a stick at the back of the figurine for the puppeteer to hold onto while moving the characters. The delicate figures look like flat, colourful marionettes with finely detailed patterns on their clothes and remarkably lifelike faces. Nevzat's enthusiasm is infectious, and through charade demonstrations and a healthy dose of laughter, I understand why this workshop is so popular.

Nevzat's passion for puppet theatre started in childhood, where he learned about the Karagoz style and technique. He later started performing in the Bursa State Theatre and writing scripts for film and theatre. Now a seasoned actor and specialist in Karagoz puppet theatre, he regularly performs shows at this museum for young children.

A school group is scheduled to arrive this afternoon for a performance, and Nevzat encourages us to stay and watch. We are pleased to join in the audience, especially after learning about the work involved in puppet making.

Downstairs in the basement a large white screen is positioned at one end of the small room. Clusters of children aged five to eight years old file into each of the rows. We sit in the pint-sized chairs listening to their high-pitch chatter and giggles, nearly interpreting the conversations just from their body language.

At 2:00 pm the lights dim, and the children settle into their seats to watch the play. The illuminated white muslin screen becomes animated with characters walking and dancing through various scenes, complemented by props of colourful landscapes and tall, wavy buildings. The historical storyline includes several humourous moments of goofy behaviour to entertain the young crowd. As the play progresses the level of energy intensifies among the characters, which are performed solely by Nevzat. Although the language barrier prevents us from understanding the full story, I do manage to pick up one word – *baklava*. Yummy baklava is one of my favourite desserts in this country.

The half-hour show goes by quickly, and after a spirited applause the children slowly buzz out of the room. As Dean and I gather our belongings, Nevzat invites us backstage to illustrate the art of puppeteering.

After a few demonstrations, he hands me the stick for one of the figurines. Starting off with a simple walk, I attempt more advanced movements like waving an arm and

114

dancing. It's tricky to coordinate the actions using only a stick, like having only some of your limbs working while others wait to be prompted. Nevzat demonstrates how he can skillfully control the movements of several characters at one time, as well as do all of the voice work. I stand there in amazement while Dean takes a few photographs of his lively presentation. There are all kinds of stages for performing, and many different roles that collectively tell a story, but my favourite is still acting on a theatrical stage using my full body and voice to portray a character in a play.

Before leaving the museum we thank Nevzat and the staff for their generosity. Dean hands them our business card to view the *Backpack Adventures* website, which will include an article about our experience at Karagoz Museum. I'm grateful for Dean's adventurous spirit to arrange this behind-the-scenes opportunity, and hope that my story meets their expectations.

It's still drizzling outside, so we grab a taxi to head downtown. We stop off at one of the tempting bakeries in town and treat ourselves to a small box of baklava. Ordering far more of this dessert than two people should reasonably eat in an evening, we can't help but devour this honey-sweetened phyllo pastry. Karagoz puppet theatre isn't the only wonderful tradition in this small Turkish city.

AMMAN AIRPORT

"You going to Baghdad?" the airport official asks Dean.

"Uh no," Dean replies.

The burly official, wearing a fully secure uniform and gun nestled into his holster, moves on to the next person in line with the seriousness of an army officer. I look over at Dean, whose appearance could pass for a photojournalist with his camera gear, khaki pants and scruffy, wavy hair, and feel a huge sense of relief that he's not part of that risky war journalist culture. He's already got a smirk on his face imagining what it would be like to travel to Iraq. I suddenly realize the close proximity we are to the war-ravaged countries we've seen on television, and feel my stomach begin to tighten.

AMMAN, JORDAN

Watching the evening news back home, I was often filled with feelings of frustration and helplessness. The international segments continuously showed images of soldiers dodging explosions between crumbling buildings, contrasted with scared citizens holding loved ones in fear. Seeing these repeated stories over time convinced me that living in the Middle East was based solely on survival, with no opportunity for creativity or self-expression.

That is, until now. All around me are watercolour landscapes, acrylic abstracts, bronze statues and stylized Arabic script with big swirling designs. The Jordan National Gallery of Fine Arts is a contemporary art gallery tucked within Amman's suburban community, and artists from many eastern countries including Syria, Jordan, Iran, Iraq, Kuwait, Palestine, Sudan, Pakistan and Algeria are celebrated here for their artistic talent.

Several works show families and communities struggling with poverty and the effects of war, but the collection is also balanced with colourful abstracts and whimsical designs. I study each piece, observing the technique and message the artist is striving to convey. In a small notebook I record the names and descriptions of a select few, in the hopes of studying more of their work when I return home.

One of my favourites is a piece called *Sand Sculpture* by Moroccan artist Omar Youssufi. Soft cascading sand spills down carefully constructed slides, like a vertical Zen garden. Perhaps it's my love of the beach that makes it so captivating. Other favourites include the bronze sculpture *Condolences* by Iraqi artist Mohammad Ghani; *Feelings from Jordan*, an abstract acrylic painting by Cyprus artist Rhea Bailey; and Jordan's Ne'mat Al-Nasser with an etching called *Dancing under the Moonlight*. I feel honoured and relieved to see another side of the Middle East that I had no idea existed.

Touring the gallery, I realize the huge impact that visual art can have for uniting people in a politically divided world. Visual art crosses all language barriers, and with an open mind, people of any cultural background can appreciate an artist's message. I believe that artists are capable of portraying the emotions, hardships, dreams and lifestyles of its citizens in a way that is much more personal and direct, and can bring about healing and acceptance in times of suffering.

I meet up with Dean and we take a break outside in the landscaped gardens, flipping through a guidebook for other tourist sites. We are soon joined by a group of local teenage girls with inquisitive looks on their faces.

"Why are you sitting here?" says one of the girls.

"We're visiting the Art Gallery," I say.

"Where are you from?" another girl says.

"We're from Canada," Dean says, noticing the look of surprise on their faces.

Dean then asks the girls, "How did you learn English?"

A girl in the front row, who is particularly outgoing, is the first to respond, "We have to learn English in school, but I watch many English-language movies and television shows. My favourites are *The Godfather* and *Braveheart*," and with a smirk adds, "My favourite actor is Ashton Kutcher."

Now I'm the one smirking, and impressed that Mr. Kutcher has a solid fan base in Jordan.

"Since I'm a girl, I like watching romance comedies, and watch Oprah on TV with my mother. My father doesn't like it so much. Both my parents teach English, so it was easy for me to learn the language growing up," she says.

The girls pass around our guidebook like it's a teen magazine, and point out the best sites to see in Jordan. They all agree that we should go to the Dead Sea, especially since bathing in the mineral-enriched mud is good for your skin.

"How long have you been married?" another girl

asks after noticing my wedding ring.

"Almost 12 years," I say, causing a stir in the crowd.

"Do you have any children?"

"No."

"Why don't you have any children?"

After a pause I say, "Because we wanted to travel, and visit people like you!"

They nod their heads, pondering the answer. The girls then notice Dean's tattoos peeking out from under his t-shirt, so I lift up the sleeve to show the full design of an Aboriginal whale. Suddenly Dean's tattoos become a convenient showcase for native Canadian art, and a way to connect cultures with these young Jordanians. Going one step further, Dean shows them the dragon design on his other arm.

"When did he get his tattoos? Were you married when he got them?" the outgoing girl asks.

"Yes, he got them after we married," I say.

"You were okay with this?"

"Yes, that's Dean's thing, so I'm okay with it," I say, although I will never understand the willingness to inflict pain on oneself with those piercing tattoo needles.

Their faces form a unifying look of shock, and girls in the back row start whispering to each other. The outgoing girl turns back to Dean's arms, now eyeing his biceps.

"You have tight muscles," she says while Dean flexes for the crowd.

The rest of the girls start giggling, and reach over to touch *Exhibit A*. It appears that Ashton Kutcher isn't the only Western man with a fan base. After the laughter subsides I check my watch and signal to Dean that it's time to go. But before we part ways the girls gather around me for a group photo. My new friends are now off to school for the afternoon.

Our next destination is the Darat al Funun (House of Arts) gallery. The twisty streets of Amman are tricky to navigate, so we ask several cab drivers to take us there. Unfortunately none of them recognize the gallery, which leaves us with a city map as our only hope. After several wrong turns and aching legs, we finally arrive at the gallery.

We step inside and discover an exhibit filled with drawings and paintings similar to the carefree, youthful style of Dr. Seuss. *Hassan Everywhere* portrays a boyish man in a peaceful, dreamlike state while floating above swirling cityscapes and riding a wave under the night sky. Many of the pieces are pencil drawings, with a few painted in vibrant blues, oranges, yellows and greens. Although the finished paintings are eye-catching, the drawings allow me to see the beginning stages of his artistic process.

I immediately fall in love with the cheerful energy of his work, and want to learn more about the artist. A brief biography is posted near the entrance of the gallery, and is thankfully translated into English.

Hassan al-Hourani was a Palestinian-born artist who graduated in 1997 from the Baghdad Academy of Arts in Iraq. A move to Ramallah allowed him to join the faculty at an art school in that city. A year later he travelled to New

York to be a contributor for an art journal, and during that time the inspiration for his children's book *Hassan Everywhere* was born. In 2003 he returned to Palestine to complete his book, however his life was cut short at age 29 when he drowned in the sea near Tel Aviv. A Palestinian foundation has since published a book of his artwork from *Hassan Everywhere*, and the Darat al Funun gallery organized this exhibit in his honour.

My heart breaks when I think about his potential for artistic greatness, and desire for love and peace in the world. If only he could have finished his children's book, pulling the reader into the kind and peaceful world spiralling in his imagination.

If only I believed that my own imagination is also worthy of greatness, without the concern of looking silly or foolish. I could be making vibrant abstract art that comes alive off the canvas, or performing scenes that open people's hearts, or writing stories that make us all value the beauty of nature and humanity. All of this is possible if I dedicated myself like Hassan's passionate journey to be an artist.

Fortunately copies of his book are for sale in the gallery, and include poetry written by Hassan that complements each piece of art. I hand over twenty Jordanian Dinars to the gallery attendant, and immediately open the book. Although I'm not able to read the Arabic script, his artwork reads like a beautiful love letter.

PETRA, JORDAN

The evening air is cool in this small desert town. Dean and I wait patiently inside the Visitor's Centre until the remaining tourists arrive for tonight's *Petra at Night* performance. The centre is spared any embellishments other than a few dog-eared maps and information sheets, but is a convenient spot to rest prior to the hike. Soon there are groups of families, friends and dedicated trekkers entering the building. My clothes are already whitewashed from a layer of sand, and we haven't even stepped into the park area yet.

Dean attempted to summarize the history and significance of Petra to me, but like many historical subjects it's an encyclopedia of information that's impossible to remember. I need to view the monuments up close in order to fully understand their meaning. Having limited reference to what I'm about to experience, it feels like a mystery about to be revealed. But the fact that Indiana Jones visited the park on his quest for the Holy Grail – now that's something to be excited about.

At 8:30 pm the tour leader announces for everyone to gather for a briefing before the walk. Once outside it's difficult to see the leader past the tall crowd, but his rules are clearly stated: avoid talking, even whispering, and turn off any cell phones. This is to enhance everyone's magical experience. At first these rules seem logical and considerate for other people's enjoyment, however with very little light to guide our way along this bumpy path, talking through our anxiety with companions feels necessary.

Apart from shuffling feet, it is difficult to sense any forward movement in this dark, still night. Up ahead we notice small paper bags with glowing candlelight edging the pathway. Not only does this help us immensely to see the way, it feels like we're on a pilgrimage.

The path soon leads us into The Siq, a narrow pathway with soaring rocks gradually closing in on us. Entering this protective cave, the candles light up wavy streaks running along the sandstone rock, which stretch up higher the further we walk. I try to imagine what it looks like without the veil of darkness.

Lumbering along the rocky path we get a peek of the famous Treasury building up ahead. My pace quickens, and with each step the narrow passage grows wider and wider. I barely notice the number of times my feet stumble and slide over stones on the ancient trail.

We finally reach a wide open space, and paper bag candles are glowing everywhere. The entire building has an orange-red glow like sunset. The Treasury (also called *Al Khazneh*) is carved into a huge sandstone hill, and the two-story façade towers over us like an ancient Greek temple. Greco- Roman style columns reach up to a carved frieze above a dark doorway. The Nabataeans Empire constructed the Treasury in 1st century AD, and remained unknown to the Western world until a Swiss explorer discovered the archaeological park in 1812. The purpose of the building remains a mystery, however many believe that it was originally a tomb.

The trudging of footsteps subsides as others gaze up at the building. Dean and I find a spot to sit down, waiting for the remaining people to arrive and get settled. The entire space is filled with a curious buzz, and a musician begins strumming his guitar. With his Bedouin robe and classical Eastern music, I am transported to an ancient civilization. Jordanian mint tea is served into small cups for all visitors, and is refreshing after the long hike.

The guitar music gradually fades away, and is replaced by the soft sounds of a flute. The music is circling all around us with no performer to attach it to. After a few moments the musician appears from the doorway of the Treasury, and continues playing while everyone sips on tea. I float into a state of bliss, then nestle in beside Dean to look up at the stars.

Shortly after the performance it is time to retrace our steps back along the path to the Visitors Centre. Camera flashes begin lighting up the dark space, and with each flash I am able to catch a split-second glimpse of the building. The crowd slowly filters out of the park, conversations spilling into the open air.

We are one of the last few to leave, trying to imprint the magical night into our minds. The walk back seems a bit easier now that our feet are familiar with the cracks and crevices in the path. Prior inconveniences have become a challenging puzzle to master, and we giggle with excitement. After reaching the Visitors Centre, we continue the climb up a steep hill to our hostel, where we both collapse into bed.

WADI RUM, JORDAN

By 6:00 am Dean and I are standing in the lobby of Sharah Mountains Hotel waiting for Mahmoud, the gregarious owner, to pick us up for a day trip to Wadi Rum. Following the popularity of the legendary film *Lawrence of Arabia*, Wadi Rum Protected Area in Jordan attracts tourists who are intrigued by the peaceful beauty of its towering cliffs and rustic coloured sand.

Frustrated with the lack of options for budget travellers, I had spoken to Mahmoud about organizing a possible tour for us the next day.

"I can do five hours at Wadi Rum in a four-wheel drive vehicle, a one-hour camel ride, lunch, and transportation to and from the park," Mahmoud says in his large framed, Tony Soprano-like personality.

That was a far better deal than any other tour group in town.

Ten minutes later Mahmoud drives up in his van with Arabic music blaring from his CD player. We climb into the back seat and hope that the ride isn't too long. I press down on the seat and gaze out the window, hoping it will distract my mind from the high-pitched music.

After two hours of racing and swerving along two-lane highways at breakneck speeds listening to every track in his CD collection, we arrive at the park entrance. Up ahead we can see glowing orange-coloured sand winding around rocky outbursts. I climb out of the van, relieved to be on solid ground, and stand next to Dean while Mahmoud confirms today's arrangements at the front gate. We then meet a local Bedouin tour guide who introduces us to our new friends.

With their tall spindly legs supporting a large rounded midsection, I wonder how I'll be able to mount the humped creature. I load up on sunscreen and motion to Dean to go first. With the camel howling and jerking its body around, Dean makes several attempts to climb on board, only to be knocked aside. Finally he manages to slide between the humps and balance on top of the beast. He can already feel the painful effects of pulled groin muscles from trying to stay on.

I hold back my giggles while mounting my own camel, and pray for better results. Feeling like I'm on a mechanical bull ride, I breathe a sigh of relief once settled on top. Luckily mine has much more patience for beginner riders. I pat his head for a job well done.

A local teenage boy guides the camels along a dusty path, holding onto long ropes in case they become too cranky. Dean and I grip our thighs together with each lumbering step. As Dean takes photos, I enjoy an elevated view of the parkland. The barren wilderness reaches for miles ahead, and blowing sand creates a soft haze around the jagged mountains.

How can there be any life here? There's no water in sight, no escape from the dry, desert air. I open up my water bottle and take a large gulp, swishing around the cool liquid in my parched mouth. Drops of sweat have also started trickling down between my shoulder blades from the noontime heat. I look over at Dean, who's pointing his lens at me, and smile for the camera. Luckily this distraction doesn't tip me off balance. The teenage boy then guides the camels toward a tent, where the tour guide is sitting on the ground with Mahmoud enjoying a cup of tea.

Following the ride we carefully dismount our camels and hobble over to the 4WD jeep. We can now enjoy the desert scenery on cushioned seats in the back of a jeep while Mahmoud and the tour guide chauffeur us across the flat, arid land.

The wind whips around us in all directions. I pull on my fleece sweater to stay warm from the surprisingly cool air. We bump along the rough terrain, admiring the contrast of rough, jagged boulders and silky smooth sand dunes. Dean braces the camera in his palm as he takes photos of the landscape. Many of the rocks have formations similar to wax drippings, and up close we see intricate petroglyphs depicting stories from centuries ago.

The tour guide challenges us to climb up one of the steep sand dunes, so we both race up as our shoes sink into the sand. Halfway up my leg muscles ache with each step, so I press down onto my thighs to keep going. It feels like I'm climbing up a mountain of quicksand under the hot sun. We finally reach the top of the dune, and our footprints quickly become invisible from the blowing sand. Tiny ripples trickle down the sides of the bright orange peak, and after a few minutes we begin the easy descent.

The jeep continues its journey around the desert park and then pulls up beside a Bedouin tent where we meet our tour guide's family. The mother and children welcome us inside, and we sit down in a circle to enjoy one of their delicacies. A large metal bowl holding a white, creamy liquid is passed around for us to sample. After Mahmoud informs us that it's a yogurt drink, I cautiously lift the bowl up to my mouth and take a sip. The drink is pleasantly sweet and tasty, and our acceptance of this offering is met with smiles all around.

Afterwards the mother shows us how they make and store the drink, which is kept in a shaded area of the tent. She lifts the midsection of a large skinned goat, bound together tightly with rope. The yogurt gradually thickens as it's rocked back and forth, and is kept cold inside the goat's skin. Watching all of this, I soon realize that I just ingested the liquid from this animal, making me almost shiver with disgust.

For lunch we stop off at a large tent where Mahmoud and the tour guide prepare a tomato/cucumber/yogurt salad with pita bread, hummus and fruit juice. They also offer a small cup of authentic Jordanian tea with a hard biscuit. I follow their lead and dunk the biscuit in the tea, which helps soften it enough to chew.

The tent is constructed using woven blankets covering most of the walls and roof, and a concrete sand mixture for the remaining walls. Mahmoud explains that visitors can book the tent for overnight stays in the park. Imagining a beautiful starry sky with the desert winds gently rocking the tent, we immediately see the appeal of an overnight stay. Guests can use mats, blankets and cushions to sleep on, and for dinner the Bedouin will cook a barbecue chicken dinner inside the tent.

I whisper to Dean, "We really need to come back to Jordan again to try our own campout under the night sky."

He nods his head while finishing off the last bit of hummus on his plate.

Dean and I help clean up the dishes and leftover food, and take a banana for snacking on later. Mahmoud signals that it's time to head back to town, so after thanking the tour guide we climb into the jeep for our last ride. Along the way we observe the residents of this small community clustered in makeshift homes at the park entrance, with children playing together along the perimeter.

@

The next day, Dean and I are scheduled to take the bus back to Amman. Mahmoud offers to cook lunch for us before we go. We politely accept the offer, even though we ate a take-away falafel wrap just an hour ago.

Mahmoud welcomes me into the kitchen to watch him prepare the meal. He chops up onion, garlic and a bowl of fresh tomatoes to cook in a pan on the stove. He then adds tinned beef and an egg mixture to the tomato sauce forming in the pan.

After a few minutes he asks me to watch over the stove while he heads to the bakery for pita shells. *Please don't let anything screw up, or I'll never hear the end of it.*

"Everything going okay in here?" Dean asks with his head popping around the doorway.

"Yeah, everything is under control," I say, while stirring the bubbling tomato mixture.

We look around at the worn pots and pans in the large kitchen. Many of them look like hand-me-downs from family. Mahmoud would rarely need to cook though, as he's hired a servant to do all the cleaning and meal preparations at the hostel. Right now the servant is probably stripping the bed sheets and scrubbing the toilets in the room we've just checked out of.

Mahmoud returns with a bag of fresh pita shells and piles them onto a plate. He carefully pours the tomato mixture onto a dish and carries it out into the dining area. The meal looks like a giant all-you-can-eat tortilla platter.

Tearing a pita shell into small pieces, he shows us how to scoop the mixture onto the bread, creating the perfect shape for maximum scoop-ability. We each take several swipes at the mixture, stuffing the loaded shells into our mouths. When I start slowing down he says "Eat! Eat!" to keep us going. Mahmoud shovels the food like a wild bear, determined to finish the entire meal. Attempting a few more bites, I stop and sit back in my chair. I cannot possibly fit any more food into my overstuffed belly. He stares back at me with wide eyes and tomato sauce hanging off his bottom lip, wondering why I gave up so soon, but manages to clear off the remaining bits in record time. He then cues the servant to clear away the mess, and we all slump back recovering from the midday feast.

MARRAKECH, MOROCCO

I can't decide which is worse – the sight or the smell. The steel grey bathroom on the train has strips of toilet paper all over the floor and exploding out of the metal bowl, and an overwhelming stench of urine. Even the toilets in first class require a gas mask, and the women standing outside shake their heads with disgust. I will need to hold it until we get there.

I return to my seat in second class, trying to ignore my body's call for relief, and watch the parched landscape stretch out for miles. Sandy greys blend into deep terracottas, with blocks of unfinished buildings popping up along the way. Seeing these incomplete buildings is strange, like an unfinished project that gets forgotten over time, making me wonder what the city of Marrakech will be like.

The name "Morocco" immediately brings to mind images of mosaic designs and rich colours to fill your home, with an earthy blend of spices to awaken any ordinary meal. Coffee table books of Moroccan décor fill the bookstores back home, and now I'll be able to experience it for myself. Like Istanbul, I'm looking forward to immersing myself in their swirling designs, adding to my list of essentials for creating the perfect world traveller home.

Our train arrives in Marrakech at 12:45 pm, and by this time Dean is also feeling the bladder pinch. We rush into the station to find a washroom, and immediately come to a halt. Cream and gold fill the spacious interior like a classic Hollywood movie set. The sun filters through a towering glass archway, highlighting a gold lotus pattern stretching across the shiny granite floor. Large white pillars sprout like palm trees up to the sky-high ceiling. Along the perimeter of the building are several boutiques and restaurants to service travellers. *If the lobby is this luxurious, the washrooms must also be wonderfully clean and modern.* I make a beeline for the women's facilities, and let out a sigh of relief at the sparkling fixtures.

With happy bladders, we sit on a bench in the lobby and pull leftover food out of our canvas bag to make into sandwiches. Dean uses his pocketknife to slice tomato and strawberries onto croissants, topped off with cheese triangles. We gobble up our gourmet lunch while other travellers walk by with wheelie luggage and stern looks. I try covering up our food and wrappers, especially since the cleaners are working so hard to make the floor shine for the next round of tourists.

We tidy up our scraps and walk outside into the hot afternoon sun. I hail one of the cab drivers circling the station grounds, hoping that he'll recognize the name of the Riad we're staying at. He shakes his head, but once I tell him its proximity to Palais Bahia, he waves his hand to get in. The ten-minute ride takes us past the modern tourist section and into traditional, rustic Marrakech.

The driver pulls into a parking lot and calls over to an adolescent boy. Blending in with khaki cropped pants and a faded t-shirt, the boy nods his head to the driver's instructions. "He take you rest of way," the driver says while unloading our bags onto the ground. I look at the boy, then at the vehicle that will be leaving us stranded. I pray that he won't lead us down a stray path to be kidnapped and mugged in a dark back alley. Dean pays the driver and we quickly haul on our backpacks for the escorted walk.

The boy walks quickly through the narrow alleyways of the medina, and broken bits of sidewalk and dirt collect under our sandals. We make mental notes of the pathway – turn the corner at the big blue door, turn right here, and follow the path to the end. The plain walls show no sign of any home life until someone opens a door. I try peeking inside, but don't want to lose sight of our young tour guide or get run over by a scooter racing by.

We reach a plain wooden door, like at a castle, and the boy rings the doorbell. *If this is the Riad, how on earth would we have found this place on our own?* Miraculously, a young man opens the door and welcomes us with a smile. The boy cups his hands for a tip, so Dean reaches into his pocket for a coin. He stares back at Dean for more, but the gentleman shoos him away.

We step inside Riad Soumia and are transformed into a world of serene beauty. Sunlight streams down from the heavens into a bowl of rose petals in the middle of the room. Peaked doorways welcome visitors into lounge areas with cushioned loveseats and a diamond-tiled fireplace. Cream and terracotta walls reach up to the open sky, and a soft breeze refreshes the afternoon sun. An ornate, wrought iron railing along the upstairs balcony decorates all sides of the square building.

Our host leads us up the spiraling staircase to the rooftop patio. An open courtyard is complemented with cushioned lounge chairs and a small seating area for catered breakfast. A birds-eye view from the balcony shows the real story of this rustic neighbourhood. Surrounding us are other tall, square Riads adorned with similar open-air patios and lines of laundry hanging to dry in the sun.

Tucked away at the far end of the patio is the Atlas Terrace Room – our private ensuite with orange striped linens on the bed, a large bathroom complete with two shower stalls, and just enough sunlight peaking through the windows to add a soothing glow to the room. I stretch out on the bed while Dean begins his new photo assignment for the week: capturing the distinct cultural dichotomy that makes Morocco so fascinating.

@

Food stall owners reach out with menus, calling out their dinner selections like midway prizes. They flirt and plead until we walk past, where the next round of catcalls begins. Long picnic tables are dressed with white tablecloths, and attentive waiters stand ready to take orders. A haze of steam from the multiple grill stations softens the bright lights at this nighttime market. The entire city is in full celebration, filling up the entire Djemaa el-Fna square in old Marrakech.

Circling the stalls, I discover animal parts that make my stomach cringe. As Dean takes a closer look, I retreat until it's only a red blur in the distance, and instead focus on the earthy mounds of dates and nuts displayed on top of travelling buggies. Crowds of people skim by clicking their cameras at the excitement swirling around them, inhaling a blend of cumin and curry powder filling the air.

We're charmed into a booth with a wide selection

of dinner options, far away from the horror show of sheep heads and mystery organs. On the laminated menu I point to the couscous with veggies and chicken, and for Dean a mixed meat skewer dish. The waiter calls out our order to the row of chefs standing behind. Steam billows up around their white uniforms as fresh pieces of meat are added to the grill. They pester each other when demand for more dishes escalates, until the boss yells at them to get things under control.

A bowl of Khubz bread is brought to the table for us to share, followed by a grilled vegetable dish, which we assume is complimentary. Dean and I gobble them up in record time, just as our main meals arrive on the table.

The veggies taste a little soft and overcooked, but blend well with the mountain of couscous filling the plate. Dean pulls away at the beef and lamb on his skewers, taking breaks to watch the hundreds of people filling the square. All the dishes appear the same after a while, similar to a barbecue festival back home. Struggling to consume the fluffy pyramid of carbs now expanding in my belly, the waiter asks if we want more. We both respectfully decline and ask for the bill.

Working out the costs on the scribbled receipt, his total of 225 Dirhams looks far too steep according to our menu selections. We didn't think we ordered that much. Dean is forced to withdraw more cash at the ATM while I question the waiter on his calculations. With the cunning nature of an experienced gambler, he points out the grilled veggies and double serving of grilled skewers that we so naively accepted. Bitterness fills my brain, wishing that I was more street smart in these kinds of situations. When Dean returns he tosses the cash down onto the table, where the waiter accepts it with a smile.

Escaping the cloud of smoke from the food stalls, we walk over to the dozens of artists in the square entertaining tourists. Women on small stools are painting henna patterns on the backs of hands. Bottles of homeopathic medicines are lined on a mat while "experts" preach the benefits of their potions to a captive audience. Monkeys are perched up on shoulders, and cobra snakes puff up their backsides to whispering flute players. Goosebumps cover my body as I hide behind Dean, begging him to protect me from the horrible snakes. He wraps his arm around me as we walk over to musicians beating hand-held drums and chanting to the crowd. Dean lifts up his camera to take a few photos, which the musicians quickly notice. They immediately slink over and flip their drums upside down, pointing inside for a tip. Dean refuses, not expecting this kind of harassment from street entertainers. Every few minutes we have to keep moving to avoid more awkward confrontations.

A small opening in the far corner of Djemaa el-Fna leads us into the souks, where we find refuge from the turbulence building in the square. The maze of alleyways in this market is a Moroccan lover's dream: floral patterned tagine pottery, lanterns in finely cut metal and tinted glass, colourful babouche slippers adorned with swirling embroidery, and an array of striped silk fabric to adorn any fashionable home. The colours and patterns are intoxicating for the artistic mind, and I want to take it all home. *How much would shipping really cost from Morocco to Canada?*

I take a deep breath and adjust my mind to finding our way out of this tangled web. There are so many offshoots from the main entrance that we start to get dizzy, but thankfully several vendors offer directions for winding our way back to the square. Within all this confusion an idea for a short story comes to mind, and I can't wait to start writing down some notes for it tonight.

Recalling the landmarks we noted for returning to our Riad, we meander down the alleyways past the tourist shops, trying to avoid tripping over bumps and stones along the way. Speeding scooters honk pedestrians out of their way, causing a flash of panic in me every time. Beyond the big blue door and around the corner, we ring the doorbell to our Moroccan paradise.

❧ Chapter Six ❧

Centre Stage

LONDON, ENGLAND

Our arrival at Heathrow Airport earlier this afternoon was full of joy and relief. Walking through the long corridors I said to Dean, "I can't believe I'm in London!" Travelling in an English speaking country was going to be so much easier, and the modern conveniences we took for granted at the beginning of our trip, like safe tap water and Western-style toilets, would thankfully be back in our lives.

The past two months have been a real-world exam in adjusting to differences in cultures, but today feels awkward and strange. Our dusty clothes are sloppy compared to the London fashions strutting by, and all of the high sensory stimulation bounces around us at a dizzying speed.

Dean and I step into an HMV store along Oxford Street to flip through London's current music scene. At first it feels familiar and exciting, but soon my eyes can't keep up. The bright colours are clashing and fighting with each other. Music is blaring in my ears. Normally it's just annoying, but today it's making me nauseous. There's so much merchandise in here that it's grotesque. It's too much. Period.

After circling the music store I meet up with Dean outside who also looks overwhelmed, and head back to the hostel to rest.

@

I arrive at Wyndham Theatre at 8:30 am. The misty April rain causes the dull, grey buildings to blend in with the sidewalk. The theatre stands empty on this drizzly day, so I sit and wait on the cold marble step. My feet huddle under me to avoid getting in the way of downtown Londoners bobbing along the sidewalk under large umbrellas.

I check my watch every ten minutes, hoping that time will move faster. I'm the only desperate soul who's come to the theatre this early in the morning to buy tickets for *Madame de Sade*, a play starring Judi Dench. By 9:15 am a few people start trickling towards the entrance. I lazily listen to all the icebreakers, jokes and usual discussions about the damp weather, trying to appear coolly interested, but the butterflies in my stomach have already started trembling as I imagine Dame Judi's footsteps touching the same pavement as my own.

With a clack of the large wooden doors, box office staff prepare for another round of ticket sales for the highly anticipated play. A few people sneak to the front of the line who want to return tickets, but after a couple minutes I also make it to the box office window.

"Two tickets in the gallery please," I say to the large rounded man in front of me.

In a few clicks I am awarded with two centre seats a few rows back in the gallery for tonight's show. The man also informs me that Judi has recently returned to the play after suffering an ankle injury, and will be using a cane on stage. My heart beams with admiration. I clumsily sign the credit card receipt, my fingers still cold from outside.

With a huge grin I skip back to the hostel, waving my tickets to Dean like I won the lottery.

@

By mid-afternoon a heavy downpour clouds my view along Waterloo Bridge. Cars whiz past me, creating an arc of water up onto the narrow sidewalk. The National Theatre stands proudly on the South Bank across the Thames River, with colourful banners highlighting the pale grey exterior and a scrolling sign advertising their current productions. It's like a beacon for acting lovers, and I've waited five long months to see some great live theatre.

By the time I reach the front doors my thin, black pants are adhered to the front of my thighs, and the clinging makes it awkward to walk. However all that rain doesn't dampen my excitement. I look around at the vibrant interior and instantly feel the energy, warmth, imagination and beauty of this wonderful place. I brush away my frizzy hair, and with a big grin walk to the ticket booth across the hallway.

"I'd like to get a ticket for the backstage tour please," I say to a woman in the box office.

"The next tour is at 12:30, and you're lucky because there's only one ticket left!" the woman says.

Perfect. That's just enough time to warm up and get a preview of the bookstore and lobby. I pay the tour fee and receive my golden ticket.

Plush carpeting in the foyer softens the giant pillars and balconies overhead, and groups of adults and children gather around a few tables. I unzip my pack and pull out a leftover sandwich to eat before the tour. All of these people can share their excitement of theatre with friends and family, but I have to keep mine stored inside. The free spirit in me wants to spin and laugh and do cartwheels around the sophisticated seating area.

I pop the last bite of sandwich into my mouth, gulp it down with some juice, and head to the bookstore to fill up my mind with educational books about acting techniques, plays, biographies and the world of theatre. By now my pants are about half dry, and the rain has eased off as well. I feel taller in this grand structure, like the ceiling is inviting me upwards.

The acting technique books are tucked within other theatre production resources. I scan through the copies, darting toward titles that grab my attention. I already have a pretty extensive collection of plays, monologues and other resource books back home, but the desire to learn more intensifies with each store I go into. I can't get enough, like the books will help me dive further into a world I so desperately want to be part of.

After flipping through multiple titles I check my watch for the time. *Five minutes – I better go join the group.* I walk swiftly back through the maze of aisles and return to the box office area. A large group of people is huddled around chatting, with the tour guide checking for tickets.

The young woman welcomes everyone to the National Theatre, and outlines the plan for the hour and a half tour. She begins with an overview of the building. Funded by the National Government, there are three theatres within the National Theatre (NT) structure – the Olivier, Lyttleton and Cottesloe. Their mission is to showcase productions that attract a wide range of interests, and the alternating production schedule provides several choices for theatregoers during the season.

I try to contain my excitement during these detailed fact sessions, but all I really want to do is step on stage. Luckily our first stop is NT's largest theatre - the Olivier (named after legendary actor Laurence Olivier). With its Roman amphitheatre style, the theatre can accommodate over 1,100 people, and allows actors to see the entire audience through peripheral vision. Our initial view is from the gallery looking down onto the broad stage, where production crews are moving set pieces around for an upcoming play.

She leads us back out through narrow hallways, past dressing rooms, and into the backstage area. A bulge forms at the doorway leading onto the stage, and I try to see past all the heads to get a glimpse. Once the line thins out we file onto stage left.

My fingertips prickle as I step closer to centre stage. The curved rows of seats cuddle around the stage, as if they are supporting the actors rather than watching them at a distance. I look back at the raw-framed set, imagining the performers running up and down the steps calling out their lines.

143

"Does anyone want to stand at the exact centre of the stage?" she asks the group.

Yes, me! I bite my lip and look around at the other people in the group. *Stop being afraid – just go!* But I stand there too long, unable to move, and someone else takes advantage of the opportunity. A teenage girl skips to centre stage and does a twirl, giggling all the way around as her friends watch from behind.

The tour guide then invites everyone up to the front of the stage for a brief shining moment. There are the usual bows and award speeches from those imagining a life of fame; others try a few dance moves or pretend they're singing to the crowd. I stand in the back watching the lively talent show, hoping the magic in this theatre will stream through my body so that I'll also have the courage to perform.

After a few minutes the group follows our guide back towards the stage door. Once the last few people trickle away, I walk to centre stage and look up at the rows and rows of lavender-coloured seats. The lights beam down onto the wood floor, highlighting the worn spots where famous actors have moved their feet with purpose and precision. My body stands tall in front of the imaginary crowd. I'm dying to break out into a monologue, to leap into a scene with other actors in a dreamlike play. I take one more look way up to the ceiling, and then quickly catch up with the rest of the group.

The Lyttleton theatre is slightly smaller in capacity, seating 800 people, but still looks massive in size. Due to a singing rehearsal we're not able to stand on stage, but they allow us to observe their preparations for an upcoming production. We all stand in forced silence while directors make revisions to the material. Dressed mostly in jeans and slim t-shirts hugging their bodies, the cast stands poised and confidently while singing high-pitched notes. *True artists are those who don't need to look the part to feel the part.*

Our last stop is the pint-sized Cottesloe theatre, situated below its massive counterpart, the Olivier. The tour guide explains that the studio-style setting can be customized according to the set requirements for each play. Fold-up chairs are placed to accommodate these changes, and on average hold around 200 people. Its simple design reminds me of the Studio Theatre back home in Hamilton, Ontario.

As the rest of the group shuffles along, I daydream back to the summer of 1985 when I convinced my parents to sign me up for an intensive workshop at the Studio Theatre. Every year, teenage boys and girls of all talent levels were invited to train their skills in singing, acting and dancing, topped off with a full musical production in its final two weeks. I had taken a few acting classes at school, but this was a program for *serious* actors.

The teachers had strict rules and serious faces. They continuously yelled out corrections during the workshop sessions, demanding a high level of excellence from the budding performers. I tried my best to keep up, but the other more experienced students with their strong voices and perfectly toned dancer bodies caught the attention and lead roles from the dark-haired Director.

They always gathered a crowd at lunchtime. I watched from the periphery with my plastic-wrapped sandwiches, composing potential bits of witty remarks and comments that could possibly advance me to the inside circle, but the risk of further embarrassment prevented too much from seeping through. I gradually faded further and further into the background, until I was merely a prop standing in the stage gallery.

My shyness increased exponentially during that summer, while my dreams of becoming an actor had been crushed down into fine sand. That experience taught me the realities of being an actor that no textbook could prepare you for. I now admire artists who have the determination to keep going even when it seems the whole world is pushing against them.

Our grand tour of the National Theatre finishes in the lobby, and the perky guide advertises the productions currently playing. While deciding which play to see I look up at the high ceiling, still feeling a strong sense of excitement and admiration being inside this prestigious theatre. Like all the actors who have worked hard and struggled their way into London's National Theatre, I cannot give up on my dreams just yet.

Following the tour I walk back to the hostel to meet Dean. With a pub on nearly every corner of the city, we visit our local restaurant for a classic English dinner of beer and meat pies. Crowds of people are huddled around watching a soccer match on TV screens, cheering for their favourite team. During our entire dinner we feel the highs and lows of the match as if we were actually in the stadium. I cannot help but notice the similarities to passionate hockey fans back home. We gulp down the last bite of food and zigzag our way out of the crazed restaurant to our pint-sized hostel room across the street.

I pull out my black tunic dress and purple cardigan from the old wooden cabinet in our room and begin my transformation from adventure traveller to stylish city girl. The twin beds leave little space to store our packs or move freely, and we nearly trip over each other getting ready. Applying eyeliner and blush feels odd yet refreshing, and I almost don't recognize myself in the mirror. I complement the outfit with a glass bead necklace that Dean bought for me downtown, and grab my small knit purse to store our tickets and keys. Meanwhile Dean finds an outfit that can easily get a passing grade for an evening out, and is standing by the door in minutes. With theatre tickets in hand, we head downstairs to join the London culture scene. *In an hour I'll be seeing Judi Dench on stage – I can't wait!*

The commuter crowd along Oxford Street earlier this afternoon has shifted into nighttime glamour, and we weave in and out of the pedestrian traffic towards Charring Cross Road. Bright red double-decker buses lumber by stacking tourists three stories high with an aerial view of the city streets. As we approach Tottenham Station the crowd becomes thicker, causing a backlog of people trying to get past the construction scaffolding on the corner. Charring Cross offers relief from the shopping frenzy, and we stop into Foyles bookstore to do some last-minute research about the play's main character, Madame de Sade.

We climb up and down the stairs of the bookstore, scouring the sections like students working on an essay due the next morning. Dean flips through a few historical books and then asks the staff for help. I stand there feeling silly that I purchased tickets for a play in which I have no clue about the subject matter. My only focus was to see Judi in person without a giant movie screen separating us. Yes, I am star struck indeed.

The salesperson graciously prints off a condensed summary of the Marquis de Sade, and his very graphic, lurid escapades while married to Madame de Sade. The play is set in Paris as it plunges into a fierce revolution, and illustrates the story of the Marquis de Sade through the eyes of six women. The nature of this story feels overwhelming, and I wonder how much I will understand. Luckily Dean is a history buff, who can hopefully fill in the plot gaps while I am busy admiring the costumes and dramatic dialogue.

Wyndham Theatre is only a few more blocks down the road, and the butterflies in my stomach are multiplying all over my body. I check my watch – fifteen minutes until show time. My pace quickens when I see a crowd gathered under the theatre's black and red sign with Judi's name in big block letters.

Dean and I sift through the crowd in the lobby and are immediately directed to the gallery seating area. The rich, opulent architecture provides an ideal preview for a play set in Paris during the 1700s, and we take a quick scan of the décor before sitting down. *Someday it would be really cool to sit in one of those private box seats like royalty.*

The lights slowly dim and velvet curtains open. Perfectly postured women are dressed in billowing skirts and tight-laced satin bodices, with hair curled and swirled high around their heads. In stern English accents they carefully control each word, further emphasized by glares that could crack the most rigid corset. My breath slows down to barely a trace of movement, and almost ceases when Ms. Dench enters the scene.

Playing the part of Madame de Montreuil in her two-toned bronze ruffled gown, Judi moves across the stage with determination and fearlessness. Her pale skin contrasts with a bouffant of auburn hair, and the sound of her deep, powerful voice causes my arm hairs to stand at attention.

She is the Queen Mother of budding actresses, showing how years of dedicated practice in theatre, film and television have refined her skills into a multi-layered performer who can master any role. I feel elevated watching her, not quite believing that it's the *real* Judi Dench on stage – the same actress from *Chocolat* and a succession of *James Bond* movies.

I'm in love with Judi's strength and wisdom. I want to remove all the rows of seats in front of me to be closer to her. I want to tear down the obstacles inside of me that keep getting in the way of my dreams.

With only a few hours to absorb the enormity of this experience, I lean forward in my chair studying the gilded cast of characters confide their deepest secrets in front of a towering Parisian mansion, further embellished by the ornamental carvings and chandelier of this theatre. As the story develops, fiery dialogue darts back and forth with increasing volume and speed. The battle of good morals and marriage commitment becomes explosive between the hot-tempered women, with a climax of lengthy, dramatic monologues.

The play finishes with a buildup of passionate, heated drama, their voices reaching high into the grand ceiling. Covering a full range of emotion, from pure joy to the dark depths of despair, I let out a big sigh at the finale. When the curtain re-opens the actors file onto stage with big smiles and delicate curtsies, reciprocated by a symphony of applause in the audience.

It was the most strenuous play I have ever watched. Taking a moment to breathe again, we slowly stand up from our plush seats and shuffle down to the lobby, feeling like we've just completed a theatrical marathon. It likely contributed to our craving for some good wholesome English food on our way back to the hostel. Two Cornish Pasties to go, please.

STRATFORD-UPON-AVON, ENGLAND

"Carolyn Daniels will be out shortly," the receptionist informs us while continuing her important duties.

As we sit in the waiting area, production workers stream in and out, checking paperwork with the front desk staff. I attempt to brainstorm a few interesting questions, but when the nerves hit creativity goes bye-bye. I stand up and smooth out the wrinkles on my clothes, wishing I had worn something more appropriate for our interview than a t-shirt and khaki shorts.

When we arrived at the Royal Shakespeare Company (RSC) earlier this afternoon, I was hoping to sign up for one of the daily backstage tours, but the box office staff informed us there were no tours scheduled for today. Feeling deflated, I picked up a few flyers about the company to save as souvenirs. But then Dean stopped me before I could make my graceful exit.

"Let's try getting an interview with the Costume Department," Dean whispered with a smirk.

Oh crap. He wants to do an interview, and tell them we're a professional writer/ photographer team. Looking back down at my flyers, I reluctantly agreed. *What am I getting myself into? What if they find out that I'm not really a professional writer?*

Dean then walked around the side of the building and opened the Stage Door.

"Hi there, I'm Dean Bradley and this is my wife Vicki. We're travel writers from Canada, and we'd like to do an article about the Costume Department at RSC. Is there anyone we can speak with today?" Dean asked while I stood quietly behind him.

"Travel writers – wow, that's really interesting! I'll see who I can find for you," she said.

A few minutes later she told us the good news – the Wardrobe Mistress could meet with us. My breathing abruptly stopped as all the muscles in my stomach pulled and cramped up into a tiny ball. I sat down on the cushioned green chair, flipped through my notebook and tried to write any kind of notes to get the blood flowing again.

Carolyn opens the large door and welcomes Dean and I with a big smile. She guides us into the dressing rooms, wig department, and the dark wings behind the stage. Admiring the racks of crinoline dresses and stiff velvet coats, I remind myself that many of the world's greatest actors have walked these same hallways getting ready for the stage. With the backstage lights turned down low, we get a rare glimpse of the empty stage. My fingers are tingling with excitement, and I turn around to Dean with a huge grin on my face.

Carolyn explains that the Costume Department at RSC has eight people on staff, including four "dressers" who each handle the costume requirements for six to eight actors. She points to a large colour-coded laminated wall calendar in her office that shows the season's production schedule. With so many overlapping plays, it's difficult to decipher the current productions. The typical 14-hour days are something she has become accustomed to, but her smile clearly shows a passion for theatre.

Carolyn's pleasant personality quickly dissipates my nerves, and the questions begin to flow naturally. Fear is replaced with inquisitiveness; confidence replaces inferiority.

"How did you get involved with the company?" I ask.

"I began my education by taking a Theatre Technical course, and then experimented in the Sound department before switching to Costume Making. I knew early on that I didn't want to be a designer, but I still wanted to stay involved in the Costume department. I worked for several years in smaller theatre companies, and then was hired at the RSC as Wardrobe Mistress," she says.

I could do that! All I need to do is get back involved in community theatre, and then...

"What are your main duties at the theatre?" I ask with intense curiosity.

"I organize the costumes for each of the productions, work with the wig and make-up department to complete the look for each of the character roles, and do multiple loads of laundry each night."

Laundry tasks consume most of her late-night shifts at the theatre. With approximately 800-1000 costumes needed during the course of the season, that's a lot of laundry! The reality of this task balances out the part of me that wants to believe that the theatre industry is a bubble of fantasy and glamour.

"Where are all the costumes stored when not in use? Are they stored at a warehouse?" I ask.

"No, actually they're stored at a nearby costume shop down the street. The staff design and create the costumes needed for the season, and then prior to each of the productions, racks of costumes are wheeled down the street to the theatre. They get lots of glances from curious onlookers!" Carolyn says with a laugh.

Once a play has finished its run for the season, the costumes are shipped to a storage warehouse. They are available to rent for film and theatre professionals around the world, and the staff is responsible for organizing and repairing costumes in their inventory. As we finish up our tour, I try to imagine the thousands of costumes worn by actors at the Royal Shakespeare Company since the 1800s when the theatre first began.

"Thank you so much for the backstage tour, we really appreciate it!" I say to Carolyn, shaking her hand with newfound confidence.

"You're very welcome! Enjoy the rest of your travels – I'm so jealous!"

She leads us back to the reception area and waves goodbye. I'm beaming with excitement as we step into the bright outdoors.

I look over at Dean and say, "Thanks for encouraging me to do this interview. I wouldn't have had the nerve to do it myself, and it was so much better getting an exclusive tour!"

He smiles back with pride, and tells me to write lots of notes while it's still fresh in my mind. I scribble down everything I can remember, not quite believing what just happened.

ꙮ Chapter Seven ꙮ

Lovers and Dreamers

ROME, ITALY

"Aaaaaah Rome, I've missed you," I say as we step off the train.

Roma Termini feels like an old friend that's come back into our lives, having met for the first time several years ago. I want to hug the station, feeling grateful for a city I'm familiar with.

We're only here for a few days before taking the train to Naples, but it's just enough time to re-visit the beautiful Pantheon and Trevi Fountain, and still enjoy a glass of red wine in the evening.

POSITANO, ITALY

"Our friends would so hate us right now," I say to Dean.

"Yeah, they would be pretty jealous. But we deserve it after all the work we did planning this trip. And think of all the amazing stories we'll have when we return home!" Dean says, taking another sip of his Blue Amalfi cocktail.

I couldn't agree more, feeling proud of everything we've learned and accomplished as backpacking world travellers: booking dozens of flights and accommodation, navigating through new cities, adapting to Eastern culture, and experiencing some of the most beautiful places on Earth, including this quaint town in Italy.

We relax into the comfy chairs at a seaside restaurant, watching the tide gently skim across the sand from our elevated mountainside view. We can't imagine a more ideal spot for an afternoon cocktail than the Mediterranean town of Positano. Even the name, Positano, has a sensuous ring to it. In the distance are cliffside homes in whitewash pastels nestled against steep mountains. Tanned bikini bodies stretch out on the beach under bright orange umbrellas, and flirting couples are lured into the ocean to cool off on this hot June day.

We finish our drinks and begin zigzagging down the narrow pathway, passing by designer fashion boutiques and sophisticated restaurants. I can't resist stepping inside modern art galleries filled with colourful abstract paintings and sculptures, wishing that I could purchase a few to ship back home. *Perhaps when I return with my exclusive platinum credit card I'll buy one or two for my southern Italian villa. Or, I could simply enjoy the artwork in these few moments and save myself the hassle. Yes, I'll go with Option B.*

A hint of salty air awakens my senses, and I skip past the remaining shops towards the beachfront. The path opens up to a wide strip of sand with loungers arranged in perfect rows, as if the ocean was a big screen movie. I gaze at the deep blue sea like a desert hiker, aching to feel the cool water soothe my parched skin. However one minor detail stands in our way – neither of us brought our swimsuits. With the morning rush to catch the ferry from Naples, I clearly forgot the part about sunbathing and swimming along the Amalfi Coast.

However that doesn't stop Dean from getting in the water. He peels off his t-shirt, kicks his shoes onto the sand and then waits for me to strip down. I stand there looking at him, wanting desperately to match his carefree attitude. The practicalities of the situation become the deciding factor – I need to cool off, but I don't want to spend the rest of the day in soggy clothes. So off come my hiking shoes, peasant top and khaki shorts. Dean smiles back at me, admitting only that he loves Italy.

We hop across the beach and let our feet sink into the wet sand. The waves sweep into shore and bring a shiver to the rest of my body. *Isn't the Mediterranean Sea supposed to be warm?* Dean pulls my arm as he wades in deeper. I try resisting, but it's pointless, and soon I am shoulder-deep in the sparkling sea.

Gliding on our backs, feeling the energy of the waves roll under us, my padded bra lifts up like a floatation device. We laugh and let out big sighs looking up at the clear sky. Crowds of teenagers splash around with beach balls and air mattresses, trying to knock each other off, while parents stay close to shore holding hands with their little wave babies.

"Let's stay in here for the rest of the day," I say to Dean.

We bob up and down in the water like otters, and then dolphin-dive to get away from the sun altogether. After an hour of swimming I almost forget that I'm not wearing a bathing suit, until we surf closer to shore. My underwear suctions to my butt as we reach thigh level and my sponge-like bra carries an extra few pounds of seawater.

We dart back to our clothes, craving a towel to dry off with. Meanwhile I try to discreetly squeeze the water from my bra. Dean giggles, and doesn't seem to mind the fact that I am half naked in this classy beach town. We then sit on a rock like lizards in the sun, hoping to dry off enough to put our clothes back on.

I hear the clicking of high-heeled shoes and conversations getting louder. I look around, and a wedding party is filtering out from a nearby restaurant. The primped young women are wearing shiny, ruffled gowns with curly hair pinned up with flowers. I feel like I've crashed their party, and try to cover up my bareness. But nobody seems to really notice, and Dean reminds me that this is *Italy* after all.

A few minutes later I slip back into my top and shorts, hoping that any remaining dampness will melt away, rather than seep through in the most embarrassing spots. As we walk along the beach I notice some landscape paintings set up on easels. The two-inch size paintings are so small that a magnifying glass is needed to see the fine brush strokes.

A scruffy man with a cigarette hanging from his mouth walks over and welcomes me to his booth. He describes his work as "miniature" painting, and shows me the various landscapes he's painted around Positano. Each one has a different perspective, including night and day scenes. He then guides me over to his collection of watercolours, and spreads out his portfolio for me to flip through.

Taking a few moments to admire each piece, he remarks, "I like the way you look at my pictures. Most people just flip through the pages quickly, not really looking at them."

Easily flattered, I continue looking through his portfolio.

A teenage girl approaches the artist with a huge gelato cone in hand and asks, "Do you still have the painting I was looking at?"

The artist nods and quickly retrieves it.

"How about seventy euros?" she asks him.

The artist puts his hand over his heart and pleads, "No, I can't, I love that painting."

"How about ninety euros?" she asks again, while continuing to lick the gelato.

Wearing a designer sundress and blonde hair pulled back neatly in a ponytail, the girl stares back at the artist. I detect a slight American accent, but try to remain unbiased during this awkward conversation.

"No, I can't. I love this painting," he says again.

"Well I have to negotiate. Ninety euros."

After a few rounds of negotiations he finally settles on her offer. She then asks if he has a tube for the painting, and trots off proudly with her souvenir. The artist folds the euros into his pocket and wipes his forehead, watching his painting disappear into the crowded restaurant.

I smile back at him and ask, "Which painting style do you prefer, oils or watercolours?"

"I really love painting in oil. That's my passion."

I hesitate for a few moments, debating if I should buy one of his paintings. Flipping through the portfolio again, I don't see any that really captivate me, but I can't bear the thought of leaving empty-handed. So I request his business card to at least remember him by.

I leave the artist booth feeling horrible. I say to Dean, "I feel guilty every time I don't buy a painting from a local artist."

Dean says, "Did you see a painting that you really wanted?"

"No, but I still feel bad....I suppose I can't buy paintings from every artist I see."

Dean smiles and squeezes my hand, and we continue along the beach strip. The sun has cooled off considerably, making it much more comfortable to walk around. We find a gelato shop and decide to share a cone swirled with chocolate chip and strawberry. The smooth, creamy dessert slides easily along my tongue, and we race to finish it before the ice cream drips onto our clothes.

In front of the gelato shop is another collection of artist booths. An older man with thinning grey hair and worn jeans greets us with a big smile and outstretched arms. With each work of art, he passionately explains his portrayal of the subjects, and then pulls me aside to look at one of his oil paintings in the sun.

"Look at how the colours change in the sunlight!" he says.

Like a true gentleman he holds up his painting to the sunlight to make sure I can see the difference in colour shades. I try matching his enthusiasm with a generous, "Yes! That is amazing!"

I return to Dean and whisper, "Do you think we should buy one? It would be nice to have a painting of Positano."

Dean nods, realizing that I've probably already answered my own question. I scan through the oil paintings, but then notice a display of prints that are considerably cheaper. Out of all the Positano landscape scenes, my favourite is a simple red beach umbrella propped up in the sand.

The artist quickly adds, "When I painted this one, I imagined a couple on the beach, but they're not in the painting since they're off swimming."

Sold! His face glows with pride as we purchase the small square print. He wraps up the artwork with his business card attached to the back, and hands it to me with his contagious smile.

On our journey back up the steep hill we pass by shops with designer dresses hanging out front and several contemporary art galleries. However I have no desire to look at bronze sculptures or wall-size oil paintings. My umbrella print means more to me than any of those pieces.

At the top of the hill we rest our packs and wait for the bus to travel back to Naples. I take one more look at the turquoise blue sea and cascading homes hugging the mountainside. I miss this town already.

BERN, SWITZERLAND

People are floating down the river like they're on a factory conveyor belt. I imagine their bodies drifting endlessly until they are found in the next town. Dean and I stand along the bank of the Aare River, watching it swirl around Bern like a blue ribbon. People of all ages swim effortlessly for about the length of a pool, then grab onto a railing to pull themselves out. Teenagers are the bravest of the bunch – jumping off bridges and bobbing up like beach balls into the swift current.

After dipping my toes in the icy temperatures I'm shocked that so many are courageous enough to withstand the arctic-like conditions. I want to give it a try, if only I could convince myself that the water isn't *that* cold.

Dean starts contemplating his own swim, and walks over to one of the stairways leading down into the water. We discover that all the entries/exits are marked with red railings, making it easy to spot while drifting down the river. Dean tells me which exit he's planning to get out, so I walk over and get ready with a towel to warm him up.

He glides in, doing a revised breaststroke to stay afloat. Within a few seconds he is already approaching the railing, chattering his teeth on the way out. I massage the towel on his goose-bumped body and take him over to the warm grass.

"It's exhilarating, even with the insanely cold temperatures," Dean says.

I ask him, "Do you think I can handle it?"

"You want to give it a try?"

"Yeah, we can do it together."

Dean stares back at me, and the fact that I'm even entertaining this idea is probably more shocking than what he just experienced. He then guides me down to the water's edge for instructions.

"It's not that hard, but when you get to the railing hang on tight so you don't get swept away. Don't let your feet touch down on the rocks or you'll scrape yourself. Then just swing around on the railing and walk up the steps. You can handle it. And don't think about the cold water, you just gotta dive in."

"OK, let's try it," I say with vigor, and we head down to the entry point.

Dawdling will just make the experience unbearable, so I try to leave all my skittish behavior behind and walk confidently down the platform steps. My toes are the first to experience the frigid water, and all five piggies curl up tight in protest. *Why am I doing this again? Nobody is forcing me to do this crazy swim. I could just as easily join all the other sunbathers on the warm grass and laugh at the teeth-chattering suckers who put themselves through all this pain.*

But then the other part of me wants to be someone who doesn't back away from a challenge, who takes the leap and enjoys the feeling of satisfaction at the end. So I repeat to myself: *I can do this. I can do this.* I step down further into the river until the water is up to mid-thigh. I can now feel the current starting to pull me in, and the point of no return is quickly approaching. *Oh my god, it's soooooooooooo cold!! How long does it take for hypothermia to set in?*

I reach out with my arms and let the magnetic force of the current pull me in. I have no choice but to ride along. A piercing chill travels through my warm body, and my teeth start chattering uncontrollably. I don't need to really swim, just a light breaststroke or dog paddle to steer the ride. Every few seconds I see a head bobbing along smiling back at me. I follow their example and try floating on my back for a while looking up at the clouds. Once the fear of getting in the water has passed, it's actually an enjoyable ride. That is until I feel the numbing effect on my skin. I take deep breaths and keep my limbs moving, trying to stay as warm as possible.

I see the red railing ahead and recall Dean's advice for getting out. With my arms outstretched and fingers spread wide I get ready to grab onto the metal railing. *I will not let this current take me away. Grab on tight!* Using a death grip on the metal bar, my feet automatically try to reach down and step onto a firm surface, but sharp rocks scratch the bottoms. I walk my hands to the end of the railing and the current swings my lower half around to the steps. Once on still ground it's an easy climb out of the water, and the warm air feels soothing on my skin.

As I adjust to the balmy July temperatures, I grab a towel and wrap it around my shoulders. I gush to Dean, "That was awesome! Let's do it again!"

Dean agrees to plunge in, but this time he wants to try a longer ride.

"How much further do you want to go?" I ask him, hoping that it won't be too far.

"Just a few exits up."

"Alright, I'll do it with you."

"Really? Well okay!"

We walk barefoot along the rough path to the new starting point. I tiptoe down the steps, and when I turn around Dean is still standing at the top. His expression turns from joy to sheer dread.

"We can do this. It's not that much further," I say.

"Damn it, I shouldn't have said anything!" he jokes, gripping the metal railing nervously.

"Come on Dean, we can do this. But we have to go together otherwise I won't know where you are. Okay?"

As I get in the water I yell to him, "Come on Dean! Get in the water!"

I start swimming into the river, looking back at Dean, and notice that he hasn't dived in.

"*Come on* Dean!" I yell, like only a wife can yell at her husband.

The second wave of frigid waters isn't any easier, but I float down the river with a smile and teeth clacking together. I anticipate the exit like a pro and have a much smoother exit.

"You made it!" I say to Dean, who's right behind me.

"Yeah, thought I wouldn't hear the end of it if I backed out," he says, smirking.

We find a spot on the grass to bathe in the hot sun. I feel the warmth enter through my pores and travel deep into every part of my body. Grateful to be on dry land, I can hear the howls of other brave swimmers gliding down the river with fans whistling at their achievements.

After reaching normal body temperature, we

decide to walk back to the hotel. But before we climb up to the main city streets Dean spots a sign for massage therapy.

"I'd love a massage," he says.

"Well today's the day you treat yourself," I say.

Standing beside a white tent with Buddha statues decorating the doorway is the massage therapist. He's wearing a towel wrapped around his waist, and has the look of someone who practices yoga three times a day, minus the trendy clothes. Dean agrees to a half-hour massage treatment and steps inside the tent.

While Dean is getting all his tight bands of muscle tension smoothed out, I wait outside on the grass and do some stretches of my own. A few rounds of downward dog help to unclench my hamstrings from the harsh swimming conditions. I then notice how many young people are walking by seeing my butt up in the air. I casually sit down on the grass and continue in a pike stretch.

Dean pulls open the tent flap and stands outside with the yoga massage man. I overhear them chatting about our world trip, and judging by their expressions it looks like the session went well. As Dean says goodbye, the masseur smiles back at me.

"So, how was it?" I say to Dean, handing over his backpack.

"It was the worst massage I've ever had," he whispers.

"What? Why?"

"He had a vat of massage oil that he poured onto me, and got way too close to my junk. If he went any further I was going to punch him."

"Really? But did he get any of your kinks out?"

"No, he just spread the oil around on me, and didn't really massage the muscles."

Dean reveals his glistening skin, and during our walk gets anxious about getting in the shower to wash it all off. In the meantime his skin is now fully primed for an outdoor rotisserie.

LYON, FRANCE

The room looks like a work in progress. I turn around, wondering if I accidentally stepped into an unfinished exhibit. Instead I see other people walk inside with pamphlets in hand looking up at the arrangements of odd materials hanging in the gallery room.

Attached to the ceiling are tangled strands of cords hanging like cooked spaghetti, forming a small nest on the floor. A few red and green light bulbs droop down in shame like a sad Christmas tree. On the wall are chunks of scrap metal and plastic hammered onto rough cuts of wood. A potpourri of blurry faces, body images and a few rusted garden tools are thrown on top of the recycled materials, strangled by cords looped around for added effect. Flags and crosses and political figures complete the bizarre message that just seems like the week's garbage hung on display.

I don't feel completely responsible for choosing the Musée d'Art Contemporain today. The city guidebook suggested the gallery in their "Arts and Culture" chapter of top tourist sites in Lyon. Perhaps the authors haven't actually seen the exhibit currently on display. Or perhaps I need to put all judgement aside and view the artwork with an open mind.

Having visited several contemporary art galleries in the last few months, I've seen a wide range of artistic styles: whimsical characters floating across the sky above swirling landscapes; minimalist stripes that fill an entire wall; dark, cross-hatched images with starving souls and overbearing political symbols; and closed-off rooms with television screens showing choppy images in a continuous ten-second loop.

However the artwork I'm seeing today is miles away from what I consider to be true creative expression. I glance over at other visitors examining the dangling wires and light bulbs, quietly discussing what they see, and wonder if there's a deeper meaning in his work that I'm missing. Circling around once again, partly to justify the nine euros admission fee, I observe each art installation with careful contemplation. I scan over the entire piece and try to decipher the hidden message behind the jumbled mixture of found objects.

After about five minutes my mind becomes so confused that I tune out all of the artwork and start daydreaming about other things. *What should I do after leaving the gallery? What time does the train leave tomorrow? Do I have all my stuff packed up?* My eyes stare into the bright lights, and their glow multiplies like fireflies in the night.

I shake my head back to consciousness, and determine that this exhibit is just another angry artist trying to make a statement about the world. I'm probably in the gallery's avant-garde, experimental section to showcase upcoming talent. I leave the room in a huff, hoping that the next art collection is the complete opposite of this crap.

I climb the stairs to the second floor. Before opening the door, I remind myself of the subjective nature of art. My opinion is only one of many. There must be a reason to include these kinds of exhibits – a Board of Directors that have decades of experience and understand the complex nature of art. *Who am I to judge?*

Glossy nature photos cover each of the walls. I breathe a sigh of relief for at least comprehending the subject matter. The first photo shows a tree branch and a bird that are slightly out of focus. I shift my eyes to the next photo, which has the same scenery but is more blurred, making it difficult to decipher the images. The third photo is the same as the first, which causes me to do a double take on what I saw originally. The entire room has repeated images of out-of-focus nature scenes.

As I walk around the gallery my pace becomes swift. Rather than walking straight along the walls I curve my path, rounding the corners. I pick up a copy of the artist's statement, read through it briefly and toss it back into the plastic holder.

Stomping down two flights of stairs, I waste no time in retrieving my bag from the coatroom and leaving the gallery. I slump down onto the park bench and look at my watch. It's now 1:45 pm. I spent only twenty minutes in the gallery, a place I thought I'd spend the entire afternoon. I swear I'll never go through another contemporary art gallery again without doing some preliminary research. However all is not wasted. The experience sparks an idea for a short story, so I take notes while waiting for the city bus.

I board the next bus heading downtown to Bellecour station. Along the way my stomach starts to grumble, so I get off to look for take-away dinner. Walking down Rue Victor Hugo I notice a bright pink sign promoting a local artist's exhibit a block away, called *Color me Bad* by Léopoldine Roux. Feeling hopeful again, I stroll past the patisserie, gelato stand and bookshop to where the gallery is located.

The small gallery is stark white, punctuated with bursts of bright colour. Thick globs of sculpted polyurethane painted in bubble gum pink spill over display cubes and windowsills. It looks like it could drip down the walls and spill onto the floor. A rounded blob sits on the floor like a beanbag chair, and I imagine it oozing out to the sides when someone sits on it.

Acrylic paintings in polka dot reds, pinks, greens, and yellows are dizzyingly energetic, blending together like a dream. A few smaller paintings show people in suits and skirts with bubble gum heads. In the courtyard are colourful cubes scattered around the lawn, stacked on top of each other like birthday gifts.

This is art that inspires me – art that makes the world a more colourful, joyful place, especially in urban areas. This pop of colour brings out a youthful energy that is easy to lose as we grow up into sensible, practical adults. There is far too much grey in cities, from concrete sidewalks to the bland cubicle dividers in office towers. We need art that feels like it's coming alive with vibrant colours and swirling designs, the kind of art that is as powerful as the ocean and as calm as a morning sunrise. We all need to feel a sense of growth and vitality in our lives. *I want to help make that happen.*

COLOGNE, GERMANY

I quietly seat myself in one of the pews at Cologne Cathedral and look up at the stone pillars reaching high into the heavens. Sculpted figures are perched halfway up the columns and multiply down the narrow nave. The heavy stone structures create a refreshingly cool atmosphere compared to the summer heat outside, drawing many people inside for a midday break. Tourists record every line, curve and design detail of the cathedral's architecture with their travel-size cameras and phones.

On the right is a tapestry of bright blues, reds and greens sparkling through the curved windows above. A group of tiny frames appear to show a story, but from a distance it has a stunning abstract design. In fact the entire building exudes a strong sense of beauty and confidence. I am one small person in this grand cathedral, and its powerful energy sweeps through me.

The energy almost becomes too much, and tears start streaming down my cheeks. The stress of travelling, feeling dependent on Dean for getting through difficult times and missing the comforts of home have caused a nasty strain in our relationship. While nine months of travelling isn't easy on any relationship, Dean and I take pride in being a good team. I don't know what to do. My heart feels empty. I stare up at one of the figures, hoping the answers will magically flow into my body.

After a few minutes I walk over to the heavy cathedral doors and re-enter the bustling city square. Squinting from the bright sun, I snake around crowds of friends, families and captivated tourists sitting on the cathedral steps. I wipe away any leftover tears and hope that nobody takes notice of my melancholic mood. Along the way I grab an order of take-away sushi at the train station plaza.

I arrive back at the hotel, throw my room key on the dresser and change into my comfy yoga pants. I find a comfortable position on the twin-size bed in the corner of the room and start devouring California rolls while watching the movie *He's Just Not That Into You* on our laptop. My mind instantly starts matching up their stories with my own. *Am I revealing too much anxiety and putting too many demands on Dean? Am I overanalyzing what Dean thinks, paranoid that he'll want to escape? Will he get so tired of me that he'll want to cut the trip short, break up and go our separate ways? What am I going to do??* Right now Dean is visiting the historical city of Trier for a couple of days, probably filling his time with much more productive activities than watching silly romantic comedies of women trying to sort out their love lives.

The next morning I go for a walk along the Rhine River, adding a dose of comfort with familiar music on my iPod. Humming acoustic melodies I notice a pedestrian/cycle path along a large railway bridge, and decide to brave the high elevation for the scenic view.

Lining the edge of the rail lines are key padlocks attached to a chain link fence. *Are people locking up their bikes on this fence? Why lock them on a bridge?* Soon there are hundreds of padlocks clustered together like stars in the galaxy. I look closely at some of the more decorative ones while speeding trains rumble across the bridge. My sweaty palms grip the barrier until the train completes its journey, but the rest of my body loves the thrill.

After exploring the city outskirts all day I return to the comforting, familiar train station plaza for an order of vegetarian Thai. Somehow boxed meals at the hotel feel less isolating than dining solo at a restaurant. I gobble up the Thai food while contemplating my evening's entertainment.

As I finish the last few bites Dean opens the door. My stomach clenches, but I manage a please-forgive-me smile. His plans to visit a museum that day didn't work out, so he took an earlier train back. A big grin emerges while Dean gushes about his explorations in Trier, visiting several Roman history sites and medieval buildings. I listen to all of his stories, almost forgetting about the turmoil of emotions I've felt the past two days. Relief melts away the tension, and I can breathe deeply again. I stand up and hug Dean, wanting to move on from all the ridiculous scenarios I've built up in my mind thanks to the Hollywood rom-com industry. Things feel good between us again, and I make a promise to always remember how much I love Dean, and how much he loves me.

A couple of days later we walk down to the Rhine River Bridge. I enthusiastically point out the lovely view of Cologne Cathedral in the distance, as well as the mysterious padlocks attached to the fence. Closely inspecting the locks we notice engraved names on them – names of lovers. Many are decorated with paint, beads, ribbons, and have a date imprinted on them.

We soon discover that Love Locks are a tradition that began in the 1980s. Sweethearts attach padlocks to a fence to symbolize their love, and once affixed they toss the key into the river. It's a love that lasts forever. *Hmmm....the passion and heartbreak of young love. I think there's potential for a short story here.*

While Dean takes photos along the bridge, I imagine the dreamy, romantic stories held tightly in these locks. It's those passionate beginning stages of a new relationship that make everyone else jealous, before the slide into ordinary routines and domestic chores, interspersed with occasional date nights. *How do you keep a sense of newness and curiosity after a decade, or twenty or fifty years of marriage?* Our logical minds tell us that we've already discovered everything about this person, leaving our hearts aching for the wild adventures of our youth.

"Want to create our own love lock?" Dean says .

"Really? That would be cool, but where would we find a lock and get it engraved?" I say.

"Yeah, that might be tricky. We can just look at all the ones here. Check out this one – they used an old-fashioned padlock to engrave their names."

"And this one has red ribbons and beads all over it. Here's another one shaped like a heart, so cute!"

Although we could search for a store in this unfamiliar city to buy and engrave a lock of our own, Dean's lovely gesture makes me feel like a young girl again and puts my faith back in love. We walk back along the bridge just as the orange glow of sunset rises up behind Cologne Cathedral, highlighting its two spires pointing up to the sky.

AMSTERDAM, THE NETHERLANDS

"I know what I want,
I have a goal,
I have opinions,
a religion
and love."

Anne Frank, April 9th 1944

Four photos capture it all. Her shoulder-length hair parted to the side with a barrette; a cardigan with embroidered stitching over a simple, hand-me-down dress; a smirking grin that plays to the camera; and eyes that invite you into the world of a 12-year-old girl. I stand there frozen in time, looking at every detail, and for a moment feel like I'm looking at myself.

The large black & white photos at the museum entrance were taken in 1941, a year before Anne's family went into hiding in the Secret Annex at Prinsengracht 263, Amsterdam. It was a year before she was forced to live with seven other people in a small apartment, with barely a whisper allowed during the day, in an effort to avoid Nazi persecution that was spreading like a disease through Europe.

I arrived at the Anne Frank Museum at noon, along with a line-up of other eager tourists standing outside the tall building. During our wait, staff handed out brochures about the museum, giving us a preview of Anne's life and the place she called home for two years. All I knew about this young girl was the famous *Diary of Anne Frank*, cherished by millions around the world and made into several plays and movies over the years. I came here out of mild curiosity, but as I read through the brochure, it became clear that her story would have a major impact on my life as well.

I begin the tour on the ground floor of the building, which was originally a warehouse and offices for the employees of Otto Frank's food-based business. During their time in hiding, Otto (Anne's father) had arranged with a few trusted office workers to help with deliveries of food, books and other important business. Today the isolated rooms are emptied of all memories except for a few old photographs and letters attached to the walls.

I climb several steep wooden staircases to the upper floors of the annex, and a large bookcase sits prominently on the landing. Constructed to conceal the entrance to their hiding place, this movable bookcase was shifted each time the helpers brought supplies up to the families. I gently brush my fingertips along the wood frame and dusty periodical cases lining the shelves, imagining their anxiety each time they heard furniture move. They could never be sure if it was friends or German soldiers outside their door.

The wood floor creaks below me as I enter the bedroom of Otto and Edith (Anne's mother) and their eldest daughter Margot. Sparse but livable, the windows are blackened so outsiders wouldn't be able see people living upstairs. A map on the wall shows Nazi invasions gradually spilling into many European countries. And like many family homes, Margot and Anne's growth was recorded with pencil markings on the wall.

In the adjoining room is Anne's bedroom, which she shared with another Jewish man in hiding, Fritz Pfeffer. Barely compatible for an older man and teenage girl, the two single beds and desk have been removed. All that remains are photos of Royal families and film stars pasted to the walls. I grin at her idolization of celebrities like many giggly girls, but also admire how these small pictures allowed her to escape into a world of beauty and excitement, while her own world was becoming smaller and more frightening every day.

The final room in the annex is a small space at the foot of the stairs leading up to the attic storage room. Peter van Pels lived in this space, the son of Hermann and Auguste van Pels, who were also staying with the Frank's. Anne and Peter spent many hours in the attic to escape ongoing family tension. A side window provided a small glimpse of the outdoors, including a large chestnut tree admired by Anne, at a time when nature was the only sign of growth during World War II.

On August 4, 1944 the German Secret Police received an anonymous phone call stating that there were Jews in hiding at 263 Prinsengracht. All eight people in the Secret Annex were arrested and taken to Jewish concentration camps. Sadly all family members except Otto Frank died at the camps between 1944-1945. Anne and Margot contracted typhus at the Bergen-Belsen camp in northern Germany and passed away in March 1945, just shy of Anne's sixteenth birthday on June 12th.

At the end of the tour is a large book with records

of all the concentration camp victims, flipped to the page with Anne's name. A lump fills my throat when I see this very real account of Anne's death, recorded in detail like it was a Census form.

I move on to other displays including Anne's personal notes and the original diary she wrote in until August 1, 1944. Writing allowed Anne to pour out her feelings of despair, isolation and wonderment to an imaginary friend she created in a diary, received on her 13th birthday. *I want to touch the paper, the red plaid cloth cover, and the indent on the pages from her pen. I want to feel her writing through her diary.* But a large glass box prevents any closeness to her work, so I try to memorize every detail before the next crowd of tourists nudge beside me.

Otto Frank was instrumental in getting Anne's diary published and making the Secret Annex accessible to the public. I watch a video of Otto describing his initial reaction after reading Anne's diary. He states at the end, "I had no idea of the depths of her thoughts and feelings."

I take one more look around the room, blinking away the tears building up in my eyes. Sadness and anger are competing in my mind, each wanting more validation than the other.

I am heartbroken, and the harm done to her feels like harm done to all young girls who are imaginative, sensitive and big dreamers. I want to protect her, even though it's impossible, and keep her dreams alive. I feel a deep responsibility to fulfill my own dreams of being a writer because she didn't have the opportunity to do so.

Before I leave the museum I stop by the gift shop

and purchase a copy of her book, as well as a few postcards. On the back of one postcard, showing the same black & white photos as the museum entrance, it reads, "This card is a special issue to commemorate Anne Frank's 80th birthday, 12th June 2009." I tuck the postcards and book into my backpack for the walk back to the hostel, feeling grateful that I had the opportunity to see inside her world a little bit more. I think Anne would be proud of how her work has inspired so many people, including this humble writer from Canada.

❧ Chapter Eight ❧

Promises

STOCKHOLM, SWEDEN

I am truly spoiled. It's my 40th birthday, and the warm water is soothing my sore backpacker muscles. I do a mild breaststroke across the pool, but after a few glides I turn and float on my back, gazing up at a large, half-moon window. Tiny white lights dot the curved ceiling, providing just enough glow without straining your eyes. Tall, leafy trees are interspersed between wicker chairs and loungers along the deck. A hammock also looks tempting, but I'm too lazy to get out of the pool.

Dean handed the spa brochure to me after our good morning kiss. Simply seeing the words "Real Swedish Massage" felt heavenly. The brochure described Centralbadet Spa as 3,000 metres of beauty and relaxation – "an open window to nature" – and the dream of architect Wilhelm Klemming in 1904 when it was built. As I read the brochure I thought, *People are always saying to visit historical sites, so why not a spa? Seems like the perfect way to understand Swedish culture.*

I slip out of the pool and dry off my limp body with a thick, fluffy towel. A few older ladies decide to test the water while hanging onto the metal railing, reminding me of the river swim in Bern when my toes could barely stand the frigid temperatures. But birthdays aren't the time to be courageous; they're for letting the spa gods pamper you until you're tipsy.

I wrap around the complimentary bathrobe and search out the sauna. I pass by a juice bar with bikini girls perched on stools and flirting with the servers. The bathrobe suddenly feels like a 1950s housecoat, and I slink by with my head down.

Although the sign clearly states that bathing suits are not allowed in the sauna, I cannot stand the thought of sitting on hot wood planks with only the steam to cover my rounded body. *And how many other women, young and old, have been bare skinned on the benches? Nope, the swimsuit stays on.*

The hot coals in the corner stove simmer away as I breathe in the humid air. I sit on the edge of the bench hoping that no one else comes in. I've never really mastered the art of saunas for two reasons: a) the awkward conversation, and b) the boredom of sitting in a hot room. I'm far too restless to sit back and let the steam melt you into a trance, so after ten minutes I open the door to cool off. My bathing suit is nearly dry anyway. I change into my undies and bathrobe and head upstairs for the most important part of the day – the Swedish massage.

Bistro-style tables and chairs are set up along the wood balcony that overlooks the pool. I wait for somebody to come out from behind one of the curtained rooms, hoping they'll recognize me for this blind massage date.

Our entire trip has been a carefully planned schedule of movement from place to place, waiting for planes, trains and buses to take us to the next destination. Constant bookings for hostels, bed & breakfasts and hotels, making sure to always be a few steps ahead for the best selection. It's been a whirlwind of constant change, and soon it will be coming to an end. After ten months of travel all our hard work will be compiled into a package of memories for years to come. I think back to all the adventures Dean and I have experienced, and how we made our dream of travelling the world a reality. An idea pops to mind about how we can best celebrate our trip, bringing a huge grin to my face.

A young man opens the door from one of the rooms, holding out his hand to welcome me. *Perfect.* I follow him into the room, and he tells me to lie face down on the table.

With only my underwear on beneath my robe, I ask, "Right now?"

He simply stands waiting for me to disrobe and lie down. *Now is not the time for modesty, and anyhow he's not so bad looking.* He rubs his hands with lotion, and after I'm settled on the massage table he makes broad, circling strokes across my whole back. The motions gradually become smaller as he tucks in around my neckline and slides down around my shoulder blades. His hands are strong yet smooth, providing just enough pressure to fully relax without the painful grinding of deep tissue massage.

He transitions from my back down to my thighs and calves, ensuring that each muscle group is fully pampered before moving on to the next one. I nearly groan when he slides his palm along the soles of my feet. Once he reaches the very last toe he asks me to roll over onto my back. I do my best to appear graceful, but in my hazy state it becomes awkward and tiring to perform this simple task.

I take a deep sigh, and he squeezes my legs like kneading bread all the way down to my ankles. After a few more broad strokes he continues his kneading along my arms, and sweeps up to the tights bands of muscles in my neck. I feel each muscle strand trying to fight back, but then his smooth hands wrap around to the back part of my neck to release. I close my eyes and allow my senses to enjoy this delicious feast that I hope will never end.

Gentling touching my shoulder, the massage therapist says he is now finished, and to relax on the table until I'm ready. I nod my head, feeling the afterglow of an hour massage, and sit up slowly. My 40-year-old body feels renewed and ready to go back to backpacker life again. Maybe I'll take just one more dip in the pool before I go.

@

We arrive in Stockholm Central Station on August 27th after taking a few days to explore the city of Gothenburg. I pull out the city map and hostel directions from the small pack, and then point in the direction we need to travel.

Dean follows behind me about three or four paces, limping along with an unbearable heavy load on his back. I remind myself that the grueling schedule and hard labour will soon be over.

We cross Kungsgatan Bridge, and the hostel is a few blocks down Friggatan Street. The bags of souvenirs and leftover food that we've carried from place to place is now feeling like an inconvenience, and I can't wait to unload them. Perhaps we can donate some food items to the community fridge, continuing the hostel philosophy of give and take for future travellers.

I look up at the beautifully ornate building and cross my fingers that it's a nice hostel. We step inside the main door, and a narrow set of stairs leads us down to the basement level. The woman at the front desk checks our names in the computer, and then insists on an extra fee for bed sheets – an unusual request for a private room. She hands us our key, and we drag our bags and sore bodies down the small corridor to our bedroom.

I unlock the door to discover the tiniest hostel room I've ever seen. A bunk bed sits along the main wall with a small table, chair and lamp tucked in beside. There's an odd drop ceiling at one end, and an exposed metal pipe overhead. It's the size of a wine cellar under the stairs, with no windows or pretty pictures to brighten up the space.

We unload the elephants from our backs and relax on the upper and lower bunks. I don't feel the usual urge to unpack and settle in, but instead pull out a change of clothes and toiletries for our one-night stay. It's too small of a room to feel comfortable, so after a few restless minutes we leave the wine cellar to explore the city.

The downtown district along Drottinggatan Street is bustling with shoppers. Today I don't mind all the modern city predictabilities we've become accustomed to these last few months. Rather than fighting to dodge the crowds, I play around the energetic buzz of people.

We find a restaurant with an outdoor patio to enjoy our last official dinner. Once we sit down I say to Dean, "Well, we did it. After all the planning and travelling, we made it happen." Dean smiles back in agreement, reaching for my hands across the table. I've spent the last few weeks aching to begin a "normal" life back home again with family and friends, but now I'm pulling back from the finish line. *Please don't let this end.*

The waiter hands us each a menu, and all of the dishes look tempting. I decide to order the smoked salmon with spinach leaves and small potatoes, topped with a light cream dill sauce. Dean appropriately chooses Swedish meatballs with potatoes. We also celebrate the evening with red wine and whisky.

I then reach into my bag and pull out a neatly written piece of paper that I've been anxiously waiting to share. Dean follows my cue and dips his left hand into his jacket pocket for a smaller folded piece of paper. Rather than dive right in, I politely allow Dean to share his news first.

<u>Dean's Top 5 List</u>

Top 5 Countries
Jordan
Turkey
The Netherlands
Cambodia
Italy

Top 5 Cities
Wadi Musa (Petra)
Istanbul
Bath
Amsterdam
Marrakech

Favourite Small Town
Arthur's Pass, New Zealand

I smile in return, enjoying his perspective of the trip's top highlights. Although I'm not surprised about many of his picks, I am pleased that he also considers Italy to be one of the best countries to travel to. I then smooth out the paper in front of me for my best picks.

<u>Vicki's Top 5 List</u>

Top 5 Countries
Australia
England
Italy
Cambodia
The Netherlands

Top 5 Cities
London
Brisbane
Amsterdam
Bern
Lyon

Favourite Small Town
Bicheno, Tasmania

The waiter returns to our table with platters in hand, wishing us a lovely meal. We eat slowly, sharing all of our funniest, weirdest and most challenging moments on the trip.

"The strangest situation had to be at Melbourne Airport, listening to the announcement about the dog chewing through the wiring," I say.

"Oh yeah. What about the time when our dopey tour guide in Siem Reap called everyone to go get breakfast before sunrise?" Dean says, rolling his eyes with a grin.

"Yes, not exactly the brightest tour guide out there.

But I think the funniest and most challenging time was staying at that horrible hostel in Kuranda. A bulldozer should tear that place down, but it sure makes a great story! That was the most fun I ever had writing on the trip."

"That's great, almost makes it worth staying there," Dean says, taking a sip of his drink.

Tonight it's just the two of us. After we return home these memories and many more will pop up in conversations and the inevitable travel advice people crave. Most of all they will allow Dean and I to look back on this experience with a sense of pride and accomplishment.

After dinner we stroll through downtown, crossing a bridge to the old section of Gamla Stan. It's our last chance to buy a souvenir, and I decide on two vintage photos of Stockholm from the early 20th century. I pour all my Swedish coins onto the counter to pay, saving our bills for currency exchange at the airport. We then slowly wander through the busy streets to the hostel, turning around for last-minute looks at the beautiful architecture.

While holding Dean's hand I say, "We have to promise to keep working on our projects and not give up. We need to keep enjoying life and not let any negativity get us down."

Dean nods and says, "I think it's important that we try and get out to small towns and special events when we're back in Canada. That's basically what we're doing now, and it would be interesting to do those kinds of things at home."

We plan to work on books, photo shows, acting

gigs, short stories, art, and anything else we can get involved in, so we don't foresee any problems with life satisfaction. The last ten months have been a great start for my writing, with many blogs, articles and short stories in my collection. We just need to keep the momentum going.

Back at the hostel and our microscopic room, both of us have showers so our quick dry towels won't be wet in the morning, and then relax the rest of the evening before our return flight home tomorrow.

❦ Epilogue ❧

I can barely contain the tears when I see my parents in the arrivals area at Pearson Airport. My mind has been primed for this moment for several weeks, but now my body is catching up. Even the heavy load on my back seems lighter and easier to manage. Mom and Dad are standing in the front row with proud smiles and outstretched arms, looking relieved that Dean and I have made it home safely from a year of travel. After rounds of tightly squeezed hugs all four of us load into the car for the long drive to their house, where we can finally see our cats again. *I wonder if they'll recognize us, or have collectively decided to stay at their upgraded accommodation?*

I roll down the window and watch the familiar highway signs pass by. I'm fascinated by the idea of being in two different countries within the same day. Just this morning we were saying goodbye to Stockholm, and now we're back home in Toronto. The space between our trip and "real life" back home doesn't seem big enough, even with the ten-hour flight and layover in London. There should be a period of transition that allows you time to adjust to the everyday life of a regular citizen.

During the past year, trends and technology have changed, birthdays and graduations have been missed, and the business world is still in turmoil from a recent economic downfall. Now we need to catch up in order to fit in. With no idea yet where I will begin job hunting, I turn my attention to more interesting topics.

With our trip behind us, we can now fulfill all the promises we made to each other. I've often dreamed about our new life – everything from our unique, travel-inspired home to a lifestyle filled with artistic projects and outdoor fitness – but it's time to make it a reality. *Can those dreams come true?*

@

Within a few weeks, Dean is back at work and we find a one-bedroom apartment. Still wanting to be close to nature, the tall complex is across from High Park in Toronto's west end. I feel grateful to have our own private space again after months and months of sharing communal kitchens and overused bathrooms. The cats settle in to their downsized home, and cuddle with us like we never left.

We begin unpacking all of our boxed-up possessions that spent a year locked up in storage. It's like we're snooping into a strangely familiar past that I don't want to fully accept yet. Beyond furniture and kitchenware, my clothes, books, craft supplies and CD collection appear dated and adolescent. I want to dump them all out and start fresh, but hold back out of practicality.

The last few boxes are filled with artwork and souvenirs we collected on the trip. Dean and I carefully unwrap and introduce the beautiful pieces into our new home. I recall buying them like we're still there – the silk painting of birds in tropical blues, greens and oranges from the town of Kuranda; the black and white poster of early 20th century explorers dressed in suits and long skirts on Franz Josef Glacier; the small red umbrella painting from our afternoon beach walk in Positano; and all the dozens of postcards, books and jewellery from every other place in between.

Once all of the art is organized and arranged on the walls, I begin my own creation. From a plastic baggie I pull out paper bills and coins saved from each country we visited, and brainstorm ways to display it on a square piece of black foamcore. Taking inspiration from the planet's round shape I start with the Australian Dollar at the top, and fan the other bills in a circular pattern according to our itinerary. Coins from each country form a smaller circle inside the bills, with a title positioned directly in the middle: *Backpack Adventures: 20 countries, 10 months, 10 days.* I proudly hang the framed art on the beige wall of our entranceway.

@

In between part-time jobs and temp work, I am drawn to writing. I read through my daily trip log, gather up all the stories I'd created during our travels, and contemplate the idea of writing a book. I stare at the two-inch thick binder of typed entries and can feel the project start to drown me. I've never tried writing a book, so where do I begin? How can I possibly choose which stories to include?

Like an organized project planner, I attach post-it notes and make lists of potential candidates. A theme begins to emerge – discovering art and adventure on a trip around the world – and after a hundred million hours of analyzing the selections and figuring out how they all fit together, the same outcome pops up every time. Intuition was right in the beginning, but my inner critic keeps flailing its arms to avoid commitment. *There must be something deeper here that you're missing. Keep reviewing. Don't start writing until you've got it perfectly planned out. Make charts. Compare and contrast. Keep doing this until you're absolutely sure that it's correct.*

Even with all the creative blocks clogging my beginner's mind, writing still feels like a peaceful homecoming. It fulfills my need for self-expression in a slower, contemplative way, and cradles my introverted personality. Although standing on stage at London's National Theatre was seductively energizing, what I really craved was an opportunity to reveal my true self. Writing can still have an audience, but I'm the one who decides when the curtain can be raised.

@

At the end of our one-year lease in the apartment, Dean and I purchase a house in east Toronto. Technically we're located in East York, but I prefer to call it "Upper Beaches" due to our proximity to Woodbine Beach. All good decisions are made while strolling along the shoreline, and buying this house was one of them. Once again we gather up all of our belongings and move across to the other side of the city, where we can now enjoy a two-story home with a front porch and backyard. I won't miss the coin laundry or slow elevator rides at all.

I soon discover all the wonderful opportunities for

water-based activities, including stand-up paddleboarding (SUP). Shaped like an oversized surfboard, SUP enthusiasts stand on the board and use a long paddle to glide through the water. The sport became popular in the early 2000s due to surfing legend Laird Hamilton, but my first glimpse was just a year ago. Watching a paddleboarder skim across the smooth waters of Lake Ontario, I was intrigued by the unique mix of surfing and canoeing.

I quickly sign up for lessons, and the moment I begin to paddle it feels like the most natural place to be, replacing any urges to become a surfer. The instructor points to a buoy in the distance for us to aim for, and I immediately challenge myself to be the first one there. Halfway across I selfishly look back at the rest of the group who are well behind me, smirking at the muscular men struggling to balance on their board.

Following a month of classes, Dean surprises me with my own SUP board for my birthday. I'm hysterical with excitement, and want to spend every moment on the water. Rather than big ocean swells, I long for mirror-like waters with bright pinks and oranges lighting up the sky at sunrise. Relaxing on my board watching nature begin the day, my heart balloons with joy and gratitude for being alive.

@

The huge task of sorting through thousands of photos that Dean took almost every day on the trip is painstaking work, but allows us to review the amazing places we visited. I love seeing the snow capped mountains of New Zealand, the Buddhist temples in Thailand and the Gothic cathedrals throughout Europe. Many of these photos were uploaded to our *Backpack Adventures* website for friends and family to follow our journey, but now a select few will be chosen for submissions to art shows.

Dean's most exciting project, however, is a book he envisioned a few months before the trip. With a fascination of local markets since childhood, Dean wanted to feature a wide variety of merchants from many of the countries we visited including the Grand Bazaar in Istanbul, Portobello Market in London, Organic Market in Lyon and the Flower Market in Amsterdam.

Dean narrows down hundreds of photos to the final collection, and I write captions to summarize the distinct features of each market. A professional graphic designer creates the book layout, which makes the entire project come alive. The final draft is then sent overseas for printing through a self-publishing deal.

Waiting two months for the books to arrive, a truck finally pulls up in front of our house. A giant crate is unloaded onto our driveway with cardboard boxes sealed up inside layers of plastic wrap. I take a video of Dean opening the first box, who proudly holds up a fresh copy of *Markets of the World*. I feel so proud of him, and want him to always remember this moment.

My love of colour, design and home décor leads me to a fair trade shop that sells artisan-made products from around the world. Its warmth and beauty draw me in, but the company's mission to help artisans in developing countries keeps me coming back. I begin volunteering at the store, and a few months later I'm hired as a Sales Associate.

The store itself is like a world trip itinerary: as Cuban music plays in the background, the smooth curves of crackle glaze ceramics from Vietnam are highlighted against raffia-woven baskets from Uganda, rich chocolate from Ghana blends in with bold coffee flavours from Columbia and Peru, and silk embroidered cushions from India brighten up the entire store. The unique craftsmanship of these artisans reminds me of Friends'N'Stuff, the gift shop we visited in Phnom Penh that also focused on handmade goods from natural and recycled materials.

During a staff and volunteer Christmas party, I disclose the steps that led to Dean and I deciding to travel the world. A small circle forms as we snack on tortilla chips and hummus, and suddenly I'm taking centre stage. They nod their heads when I describe our love of travel, but when I recite the "What I Want" list from my office admin days, everyone's eyes light up and a buzz of inspiration takes over. *I want energy....... I want positive spirit....... I want artistic freedom..... I want to be set free and fly around the world...... I want to experience a bigger, more fulfilling life.* Those words feel like a lifetime ago. The magic of that fateful day still amazes me, and how simply writing down your wishes can help you realize your dreams.

When I arrive home from the party, I go straight to my laptop and begin typing a new set of goals for myself. Like the previous list, these points flow freely onto the page:

I want the courage to follow my curiosity wherever it takes me

I want to feel free to express my creativity in many ways

I want to make time daily to focus on my creativity

I want to share my creativity with others

I want to feel proud of who I am

I want to give thanks daily

I read over the list and immediately notice a change of perspective and temperament. Five years earlier I craved a jolt of excitement and rebellion to set me free into a bigger life. I believed that I could only fulfill my dreams by leaving home. My current goals show a much softer approach to creating the life I want through exploration, dedicated practice and gratitude.

I print off the page and tuck it in my drawer, hoping that the same magic will happen once again.

Dean and Vicki's World Trip 2008-2009

Countries Visited:

Australia	Morocco
New Zealand	Spain
Thailand	Italy
Cambodia	France
Vietnam	Switzerland
Egypt	Germany
Turkey	Czech Republic
Jordan	The Netherlands
England	Norway
Scotland	Sweden

Links to Arts and Cultural Attractions:

Sydney Opera House:
www.sydneyoperahouse.com

Nelson Bone Carving:
www.carvingbone.co.nz

Jim Thompson House:
www.jimthompsonhouse.com

Friends Restaurant, Friends 'N' Stuff:
www.mithsamlanh.org

Jordan National Gallery of Fine Arts:
www.nationalgallery.org

Darat al Funun gallery:
www.daratalfunun.org

National Theatre, London:
www.nationaltheatre.org.uk

Royal Shakespeare Company:
www.rsc.org.uk

Musée d'Art Contemporain, Lyon:
www.mac-lyon.com

Anne Frank Museum:
www.annefrank.org

❧ Acknowledgements ❧

To Chris Kay Fraser of Firefly Creative Writing for her dedication and amazing insight during this entire project. I could not have accomplished this book without her support.

To my Dad for his guidance and feedback on this project, and taking the time to answer any nagging technical questions on the writing craft. To my Mom for her unwavering love and support over the years, and offering comfort during the most challenging times. To our friends and families for their love and understanding, and keeping us updated on important news and events happening back home.

To the staff and volunteers at Ten Thousand Villages Danforth, for listening to many of my travel adventures and whose encouragement for writing a travel memoir has been greatly appreciated.

To all the people I met around the world, who have inspired me with their stories and smiles.

Most of all to Dean, who was loving, encouraging and dedicated in every way during this yearlong adventure, and whose photos have created a beautiful lasting memory of our trip.

CPSIA information can be obtained at www.ICGtesting.com
Printed in the USA
LVOW07s0212250315

431858LV00008B/62/P